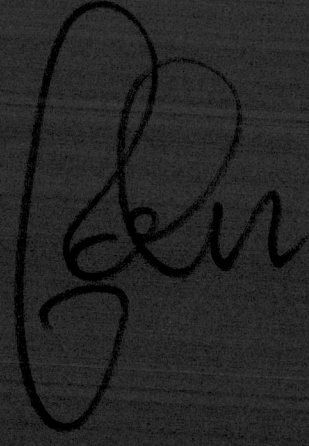

This book is dedicated to my beautiful daughter Rebecca and my lovely granddaughter, Sophie.

THE BEST OF TIMES

Typeset and printed by:
MTP Media Ltd | The Sidings | Beezon Fields | Kendal | Cumbria | LA9 6BL
Reg in England: 06491633   Telephone: 01539 740 937   www.mtp-media.co.uk

First published in May 2023

Copyright © John Lockley & Jocky Sanderson
thegoldenrule.com   jockysanderson.com

John Lockley asserts the moral right to
be identified as the author of this book

All rights reserved no part of this publication may be reproduced, stored in a retrieval system, or transmitted, in any form or by any means, electronic, mechanical, photocopying, recording or otherwise, without the prior written permission of the publishers.

Cover photograph by Rob Grange.   robgrange.co.uk

Back page photographs:
John Climbing on White Ghyll, by Bill Birkett   billbirkett.com
John in the cellar, by Flash Birkett

Acknowledgements

Russel Mills and Deborah Walsh

Bill Birkett

Nick Fieldhouse

Jocky Sanderson

Katherine Wilson

Rebecca Lockley

Paul Renouf

David Miles

Andrew Leatherbarrow

Rob Grange

Hope Elegia Wandless

John Wrennall & the great team at The Golden Rule

All my dear friends and customers for all the support
and encouragement they gave me while writing this book.

Contents

FORWARD		1
CHAPTER 1	The Early Years	5
CHAPTER 2	Grammar School, 1955	15
CHAPTER 3	The Gondola	19
CHAPTER 4	The Move South	23
CHAPTER 5	The Farming Years	25
CHAPTER 6	The Bull	29
CHAPTER 7	New Knee	43
CHAPTER 8	The Golden Rule	63
CHAPTER 9	Hangover	77
CHAPTER 10	Ballooning Years	95
CHAPTER 11	Mexico — To Find My Father	109
CHAPTER 12	Thank You	115
POEM — The Golden Rule		118

Forward

I first met John in 1989. Back then, paragliding was a lonely adventure sport, with few of us flying in Cumbria. I was soaring and watched John pull up and emerge from his Citroen 2CV dressed in his fleece, and Ron Hills tucked into his Nokian wellies. I was to learn this was to be his chosen attire for every occasion for the next four years. We shared the open sky, soaring above Bewaldeth, laughing and screaming at each other, and from that day on, we became inseparable friends.

When we first met, John had recently turned his back on alcohol. I felt it important to assist him in his distraction by continually calling him up with a variety of challenging ideas and cunning plans, from attaching a paraglider to a windsurfer during a storm, to trawler fishing in Skye. John would always say "aye, all right." He always reminds me of that great quote, "that is a terrible idea, what time?"

John has an uncrushable enthusiasm and willingness to give anything a go. This can sometimes get him in trouble, as the stories in his book will testify, but in general his jovial smile and positive approach to situations and people would seem to always have him and his fellow cohorts scraping by with a relieved "phew, well that was fun" conclusion.

Aside from flying John has always loved climbing, his pub 'the Golden Rule', and spending time with his lovely wife Margaret and their daughter Becky. John's twin brother Phillip has always been an important part of his life. Even to this day you can set your watch by Phillip's 09:30 Sunday morning call. Having a strong family and circle of friends have given John a stable, secure base to enable him to pursue his dreams and do what he's always loved doing: to play and be free. And, of course, he shared his tales of adventures so openly with locals and new customers alike at the Rule, always with his infectious smile.

During the Covid years, this free spirit was caged. For the first time I saw John sad and frustrated, trapped and apart from his much-loved customers and friends. He decided to write a journal of his life, a project which has snowballed. John wrote page after page on scraps of paper that would often fall all over the place, and once the pub was allowed to re-open, he'd scoop them up and proceed to hold court reading chapters to his customers once again. Over time, we started to convert the wonderful scraps into typed text and collected photographs from albums and the walls of the pub to compliment his great tales.

As John's journal evolved, folk have tried to help by correcting his writing style. But for us, to celebrate the real John Lockley, "honesty, warts and all," it was important that his words were left as his own, as they represent his thoughts best. John would be the first to admit he was no Shakespeare, but we hope his honesty and love for life comes out through the pages of his humble book.

For those lucky enough to have met him, we all know John is a larger than life, kind and magnificent man. I am sure we are united in enjoying taking a little time out of our lives to enjoy John's warming and humorous journey through these pages.

Jocky Sanderson
Keswick, UK
March 2023

The winter of 47 was really bad. The snow went half way up the telegraph poles and it froze and snowed for weeks.

It was at this time that I became aware of having an elder brother, Andrew. Father had a sledge made for us at Vickers. It was the rolls royce of sledges and went like the wind

Andrew was the sledge master, and we sat behind, he had no fear, and at 7 years old was destined to be a leader.

Our cousin Leslie and his mum Alma lived with us at this time. His father also Leslie had been killed when on a bombing raid over Germany. He didn't know that Alma was pregnant at the time, poor chap.

His remains lie at Illogan in Cornwall, Phillip lives near there and whenever I'm in Cornwall, we go and pay our respects to him.

On those cold nights, we would sit by the fire and listen to the radio. Taggy the cat would be there, but he fucked off, because we kept pulling his tail.

Glaxo had come to Ulverston to process penisyllin at this time, and the council were building a big estate to house the new workforce. This became a great adventure playground for us kids, and was our first introduction as very junior members of a gang.

Father was doing well at Vickers, so with a loan from Dana, our maternal grand ma, he purchased a large Victorian house in Town "Beechbank, it cost £1800. A new chapter.

CHAPTER 1

The Early Years

Ah well, I was introduced to this world September 18, 1944. It was the battle of Arnhem, and like mother, the troops were having a bit of a struggle. The reason for this was that Phillip (my twin) arrived twenty minutes after me. He was not expected, to the surprise of everybody, except me.

We lived at Rakehead, in the outskirts of Ulverston which was then in Lancashire. The house was a semi, which was rented from some distant wealthy relations.

I don't remember too much of the early years but some things stand out, like the time Phillip and I found a tin of green paint. The whole road got decorated, trees, walls, garden gates, the lot. We were apprehended by next door neighbour Jim Siddall who worked with father at Vickers Armstrong in Barrow. He sat us down in his greenhouse which smelt of tomato plants and tobacco, and told us how bad we had been. I also remember us having a see who could piss up the wall competition with a girl who lived down the road.

We were naughty boys, so mother decided that we went to school, we were three years old and Dale St. School was one and a half miles away. Mother took us on the first day. On the next morning, we were on our own, and lost our way, a kind council worker with a horse and cart gave us a lift and dropped us off at school (a kind man).

Cod liver oil and orange juice was the order of the day, and now leads us to the dreadful winter of 1947. The winter of 47 was really bad. The snow went half way up the Telegraph poles and it froze and snowed for weeks.

It was at this time that I became aware of having an elder brother, Andrew. Father had a sledge made for us at Vickers. It was the Rolls Royce of sledges and went like the wind. Andrew was the sledge master, and we sat behind, he had no fear, and at 7 years old was destined to be a leader.

Our cousin Leslie and his mum Alma lived with us at this time. His father, also Leslie had been killed when on a bombing raid over Germany. He didn't know that Alma was pregnant at the time, poor chap. His remains lie at Illogan in Cornwall, Phillip lives near there and whenever I'm in Cornwall, we go and pay our respects to him.

5

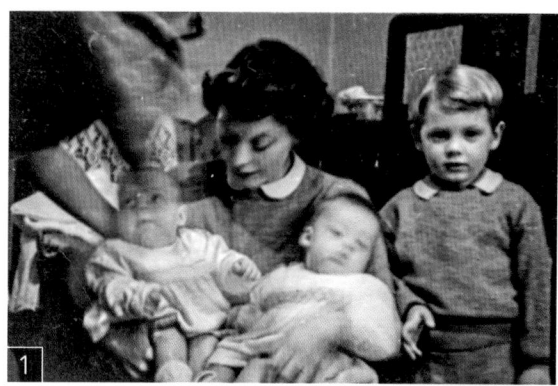

1   Proud Mother with twins while Andrew looks on
2   The brothers grim
3   Feral boys
4   Father in Moscow
5   Father building the patio at Beachbank, Ulverston

6   Mother with lion cub at Whipsnade Zoo
7   Mother & father at their wedding in 1939
8   Dorothy Scorer, Dana, Leslie Cousins, Mother, Father, Dan Dan, Aunt Alma, Grandma Lockley
9   Mother holding baby Andrew

On those cold nights, we would sit by the fire and listen to the radio. Taggy the cat would be there, but he fucked off because we kept pulling his tail.

Glaxo had come to Ulverston to process penicillin at this time, and the council were building a big estate to house the new workforce. This became a great adventure playground for us kids and was our first introduction as junior members of a gang.

Father was doing well at Vickers, so with a loan from Dana, our maternal grandma, he purchased a large Victorian house in town, 'Beech Bank', it cost £1800. A new chapter. Beech Bank was a fine big Victorian villa, in a nice elevated part of town, close to the parish church. It was on the end of a terrace of four, all very middle-class, really quite grand! My parents were obviously on their way up, so at this point, I should write something of them, and their lives.

Father came from a large poor working class family in Birmingham. He had a lovely singing voice, and was noticed by Bishop Pelham, the last bishop of Barrow. The old bishop took father on as his ward. He brought him to the rectory and to St Cuthbert's church in Aldingham, a beautiful hamlet right on the north shore of Morecambe Bay, between Ulverston and Barrow. This little church has had a family significance since that time. The bishop educated him, mentored him, and introduced him to local society (father's first step up).

Mother and Alma were born in London, her father was an American artist, fine art dealer, and entrepreneur. He came from a farming family with eight siblings, and they were from Illinois. He was the resident artist with the Canadian Pacific railway when it was being built. It is said that he imported two roller skating rinks from America and through this he met Dana (mother's mum). Dana was a dancer, and it is believed she taught Charlie Chaplin how to roller-skate. She and Bekker married in 1914, mother was born 4 months later. Dana was 23 he was 51. They lived in Fulham but in 1917 the family moved to Barrow, where Bekker was to paint scenes of the Lake District, but the poor bugger died in the December of that year. Mother inherited her father's artistic skills, and had a great talent, even winning a first prize in a Daily Mail competition, and teaching art at night school.

I think it was 1948 when we were established at Beech Bank. Phillip and I started a new school, Church Walk infants, 5 minutes from our new home. We were very upset that day, and cried and cried until mother was phoned to come and take us home. Yes, we had a telephone then. Ulverston 2350. The school was pretty nice, a little bit rural with decent kids and parents. One thing I do remember is coming home one afternoon, I was bursting for a shit, but try as I might I couldn't hold it back so I shat myself and got home embarrassed and a bit smelly. Aunt Almer was there, so she was given the job of sorting me out, she was kind, and told me that all children did it from time to time, bless her.

Another little problem I had, was wetting the bed. Andrew took great delight at this and gave me nicknames such as The Ringmaster, or 'Dampium wettum.' He had started taking swipes at people. He once caught Ma and Pa in the bath together, so he named father 'lighthouse,' and mother 'seaweed.' He was clever but wicked and cruel.

Father's career was going well, and he started to spend more time abroad doing trade deals and making commercial contacts. Mother was in charge, but could not control us boys, we became feral, out all the time. We had a wonderful time roaming about the woods and moorlands that surrounded Ulverston. Andrew or Andy as he was called, was becoming more assertive as gang leader. He used the cellars in the house as his H.Q. I would get a note telling me that I had an appointment at the "Vunderheim," when little acts of cruelty would be meted out on me. I would get into bed only to find a couple of grass snakes in there, or walking along with the boys, finding that frogs had been carefully placed in my pocket. One day they grabbed me, tied me by the wrists and ankles, hung me upside down from a fir tree, so that my head was about 2 feet from the ground, then cut the rope. That fucking hurt, but they thought it was hilarious.

On Sunday afternoons, we were sent to Sunday school. I suppose it gave the parents a chance to have some time to themselves. On this particular day, Andy was tasked to go with us to the Parish Hall. Andy was having none of this, we were to go adventuring instead. Within an hour, it started to rain, Andy looked skyward and shouted, "You blithering blockhead God." This worried me a bit, it didn't seem right. Aunt Alma had re-married to John Cummings. He was a war hero, ex-commando, and headmaster of Leytonstone Grammar School in Essex.

The family would drive up from London at the start of the summer holidays, Leslie would be dropped off at Beech Bank when we boys would be lined up to receive half a crown each.

Uncle John looked up into the copper beech tree at the bottom of the garden, and was horrified to see three dead toads suspended side by side. Andy had hung them (that was the norm to us). Leslie was left to settle in with us, and the Cummings family went on to Barrow, where John's mother and Dana lived. Old Mrs Cummings was a bit scary, she looked like the ageing Queen Victoria, all dressed in black and very stern! Whilst Dana was very different, she was good fun, and would often come on long bird nesting walks with us boys and our two corgis Miffy and Minky. Even Simon, the siamese cat, would sometimes join us on these expeditions.

Behind the house was a large walled garden we called the private ground. Father grew potatoes, raspberries, sprouts, strawberries, and was a good gardener but his trips abroad became more frequent, his husbandry diminished and the garden became our headquarters. He was in Moscow when they launched Sputnik. He loved it there and even gave interviews on Radio Moscow, being told what answers to give to each question.

Across the lane from the garden was Stalker's field. Mr Stalker was a coal-man and kept his horses there. Those poor horses would come to the gate to see if we had anything for them. We certainly had: mustard sandwiches. They looked so funny once they had eaten them. They would roll their eyes, flair their nostrils, and put out their tongues and blow air through them to cool things down. We would howl with laughter at those poor beasts. Often they would stand at the gate when their big old cocks used to hang down. This was too much of a temptation for us. We had catapults, so those big old cocks became a target. A hit would result in a hasty retraction, and the poor horse to gallop off.

Behind the private ground wall lay a holding of gardens, hen houses, and fruit trees, and directly below the wall was a huge sandpit in which we would play. This belonged to Mr Moon, who was an electrician at Vickers. He would sneak up on us armed with cable with which he would swat us, and by gum, that stung! We would be back over that wall like rats up a drainpipe. We got our own back though, once dark, we would go back and pinch his apples, (his nickname was flex).

Phillip stocked private ground with banties, guinea fowl, pheasants, you name it! The rhubarb patch was occupied by captured grass snakes, an area to be avoided by me. The neighbours started to complain about the noise the cockerels would make in the early hours, so father told Phillip to get rid of some of the birds, or he would have to cull them. "Idle threats," said Phillip. The next day, father appeared with an axe. I caught the offending birds, held them down and pa chopped their heads off. "I'll give him idle threats," said dad. For the more exotic birds we kept, dad built us an aviary in the back yard. So many different breeds of budgies and canaries dwelled within, although the zebra finches were allowed to live in the breakfast room. At this point, I must write about Bill.

Danna took Phillip and I to Walney Island and on the beach we found a young razorbill all covered in oil, and very weak. Phillip gathered him up and onto the bus we got. We had to change buses at Barrow town hall where there was a market. As we passed a fishmongers stall, young "Bill" found it too much to resist, and having wriggled from Phillips grasp, he jumped onto the counter and started to help himself to the fresh sprats on display. You can imagine what the man said. We took him home, cleaned him up and he became a dear pet. We could take him to the beach, let him have a swim around, and he would be happy to come home again with us, swimming in our bath, being fed sprats that we had to buy. Sadly, Bill got caught up in a bicycle wheel, and necked himself.

Another memorable pet was "Twit," a fledgling Tawny Owl who Phillip found in Old Hall Wood. She became a favourite, and would come and go as she wished. She roosted in the breakfast room on the clothes rack over the oven. The zebra finches didn't think much of this, but all seemed to go well. One day, Twit came to school with us (at this point, I should say that we were about 8 years old, and at Primary School). Mr Chadwick, the headmaster, was writing on the blackboard, one of those wall mounted boards that nearly went the width of the room. Twit was now sitting on Phillip's desk, Mr Chadwick writing, the class in utter silence, and wondering what next. Twit took off and flew silently, as owls do, and perched above Mr Chadwick's head. He kept writing, the class kept silent. Twit turned his head to observe us bemused pupils. Then shat, straight down the blackboard, next to Mr Chadwick. The class erupted, poor Mr Chadwick was a bit shocked, but took it in good heart.

Primary school is a kind of a right of passage, new friends, new enemies. One learned self expression, how to fight, if one had to, and how to take punishment bravely. We were often punished because we were often naughty. Phillip and I were known as the Terrible twins. Often, we would be hauled before father by angry neighbours, who we might have robbed,

1 Studio photograph of the young brothers
2 Young twins at 6 years old, post the strawberry event

or let their tyres down. We thought it such fun!

Mum and dad were very social and quite middle class I suppose. We had a Chinese themed drawing room with black lacquered furniture and a Chinese carpet. Mollie Marsh, a friend of mums came for tea one day. Mum had painted a large Mural on an alcove wall, it was pretty good. Mollie was admiring the work, when Phillip came in with his favourite broody pigeon. This is Celia, said Phillip. Celia then fluffed up her feathers, and shat the biggest turd you could ever imagine from a bird that size. Plop, right onto the Chinese carpet. Mollie Marsh uttered only one word, "Gosh."

Andrew was now going on 12. He was quite wild, and the parents decided he would have to go to boarding school. So off he went to Bentham Grammar School. Lots of middle class kids were sent to boarding school in those days. Phillip and I scraped through our eleven plus and so went to Ulverston Grammar School. Prior to this, I joined the Parish Church Choir. My brothers thought me soft, but I quite enjoyed it. I think there was a spiritual side to me that lifted me. Father had a very rich bass voice and he encouraged me. They wanted me to go to a London choir school, but I wasn't up for that.

Aunt Margo was a big woman, big in every sense — big hearted, a very hefty 18 stone, but very personable, and rather beautiful. She had great style, and commanded attention from everyone around her. She was cousin to Leslie Cousins, Aunt Almas first husband, who died whilst serving in the RAF, so not an aunt to us in the real sense, but a proper member of our family no less. As the school meals supervisor for Lancashire, she had a new car every year, always an Austin. This car was at our families disposal whenever father wanted. I think she was in love with father, but her great sense of morality kept her feelings hidden (I think father knew). She lived near us in Ulverston, with her mother, Aunt Jessie and her aunt, Aunt Florrie at the weekend, but in the week she had a huge flat in Lancaster.

For a treat, she would take Phillip and me to Blackpool Tower Circus. We would be put on the train in Ulverston, she would meet us at Lancaster, then whisk us off to Blackpool for an enchanting evening the famous "Tower Circus." Then back to Lancaster where she would cook us a wonderful supper, including ice cream, which she would make herself. Then to bed, and a splendid breakfast next day. She could cook, that woman, and was so very kind to Phillip and me. Margo's father, Dr Cousins, was the first headmaster of Ulverston Grammar School when opened in 1932. An academic, he had been headmaster at Alston prior to coming to Ulverston. He wrote a definitive book on Beekeeping and died in 1940.

I write about Aunt Margo at this stage of my life, but the reader will find that she pops up throughout my life, until her sad death in 1991.

One evening, when I was about ten, I was walking on my way down the garden, on my way to choir practice when I met father coming towards me. He looked distressed and I saw he was carrying Ghilly, our little terrier. "What's up dad," I asked. "Ghilly's dead," he said.

And I noticed tears rolling down his cheeks. The little dog had slipped his lead and was run over by a car. This was the only time I saw my father cry.

1   Dear Aunt Margot
2   Mother looking innocent
3   The author with Twit

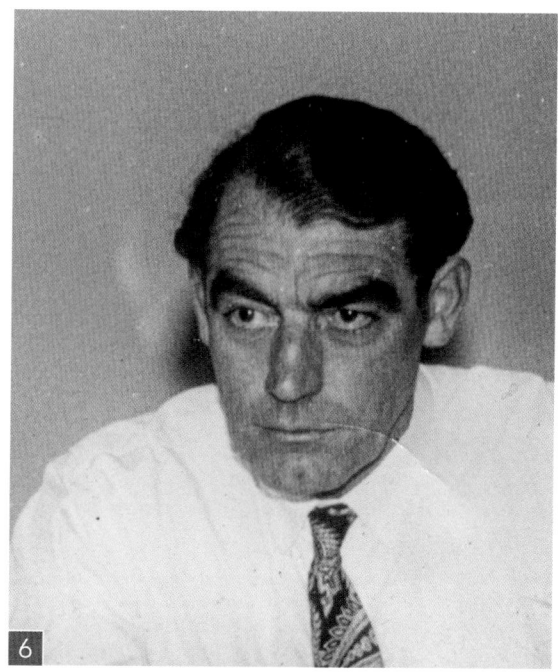

4   Mother and father walking wedding
5   Alma and mother (standing)
6   Father in a meeting at Vickers

CHAPTER 2

Grammar School, 1955

So, during a wet summer holiday, we went camping at Fell Foot, which is at the southern end of Windermere, just above Newby Bridge. I remember father digging trenches round the tents to redirect the flood in an attempt to keep us dry in our soggy temporary homes. Andy got stung by a hornet, which had gone down his wellington. This happened as we released a load of minnows we had caught into the flooded foundations of a huge mansion, the building of which had been abandoned.

To Catch Minnows

Take a wine bottle, punch a hole at the base where it is concave, put a load of bread in the bottle, capture a length of string with the cork at the neck, drop it in the lake, then wait for nature's bounty.

Once the weather had greatly improved, it was time to go to the Grammar School, with our caps, blazers, badges, and school tie. All very smart, but the thing was, to try to look as scruffy as possible and get away with it.

The headmaster was called George Longbothom, his nickname was "Drag." He was a friend of father's, and said to me, "Your father has given me permission to beat you as often as I think necessary," and the fucker did. We deserved it most times, he was an okay chap really.

The Grammar School was a real eye-opener to us lads, students came from miles around from Coniston and Hawkshead in the north, Cartmell and Grange-over-Sands to the east, and Broughton and Dalton to the west. We were about 1000 students.

There were girls, of whom we knew little apart from early innocent friendships. There were hoards of them in all stages of their pubescence. All of a sudden, we were growing up, the first few weeks were quite confusing as we navigated the geography and the mechanics of how the place worked.

As newcomers, we were at the bottom of the pecking order, older students were held in awe, especially the prefects, who were almost godlike. Some were helpful in a condescending sort of way, some treated us like we were dog shit on their shoes, "go away child." One or two of the guys were just bullies, we soon found out who to avoid.

New friendships were now being forged as quite a few of my old pals went to the secondary modern school. We thought they were thick, but I know now that is not the case.

Bill Wallis was the head there, a short fat Yorkshire man, with a bald head. He liked toast and dripping (beef fat). I remember Bill and Joan were friendly with my parents. I would stay with them when the folks went away. I remember once they went to Belgium and Holland with Aunt Margo in the Austin, of course.

Pa taught Bill to drive, I remember, I was in the back seat of Bill's new Ford Prefect. The car set off in a kind of bouncing jumping motion, it was a job staying on the back seat.

I was still in the choir at the Parish church at this time. I had a good voice, but Mr Pilkington, the music teacher from school, found this out. He would get me to sing solo soprano parts in front of the school. I hated it and couldn't wait for my voice to break.

Phillip and I didn't care much for academia, the great outdoors was where we wanted to be. We were still feral, and a gang of us would roam the countryside on our bikes. One day, we set fire to the gorse bushes on Hoad hill, we thought it great fun as we watched the fire brigade trying to put it out. It would not be long before we grew out of these childish things.

Phillip had a pal called Pete Aiery, his dad had a farm at Cartmel and Phillip would go to help out there, and on Sundays we would go there shooting. Nothing was safe.

I started to help out at a farm at Newlands, a hamlet next to Ulverston, which was run by two brothers, Noel and Bernard Butterfield, under the watchful eye of their mother Nellie. There I learned a lot. How to milk cows, how to make up rations for them, we cut kale and pulled mangolds in winter.

The Butterfields lived quite a frugal life. One day, we were carting bales of hay into the barn, and I noticed a dead hen floating in the water trough. Sure enough, it was chicken for lunch the next day. The cooking was done on an old fashioned range, and the sausages were never properly cooked. I could barely eat them, but was too polite to leave them.

We would cut bracken for bedding and cut grass for hay in summer. At 13 I was a competent tractor driver and cow milker. We were paid for the work we did, and with the pocket money we were able to extract from dad we were quite affluent. I think he gave us five shillings a week.

Most of the clothes we wore were hand-me-downs from the older children in our parents' social circle. Underclothes were not included. One day father got us some underpants, I think they were ex-army. They were so awful that we refused to wear them. I think this was our first challenge to his authority. We were fourteen by now, and one had to be wearing, I think it was Y-fronts at this time.

By now we had girlfriends, who we would take to the pictures, and to parties, or the dances they had at local village halls. Now the boys would score the girls as to what favours they would grant us. One for a kiss, two for a kiss with tongues and so on. Some boys would say they got to No. 10, but they were generally lying, not good for a girls reputation.

During this time, Andrew had come back to the Grammar School to do his A-levels. He soon settled in and knocked about with a bunch of guys who saw themselves as a bit superior. They would wear sports jackets, cravats and suede shoes. They would strut about school as if they owned the place.

Andrew joined the Territorial Army and he showed great promise. He was obsessed with weapons, so we had rifles and shotguns always in the house. He loved fly fishing and was quite good at it.

As Ulverston sits at the head of the canal right on Morecambe Bay, we were always on the sands, fishing and wild fowling. Nobody bothered in those days about us young lads carrying weapons, I often used to take the bus to Torver carrying a shotgun.

Pete Whitfield, a mate from school lived at Torver at a place called Brackenbarrow. His step father was an architect and his mother came from Wales. They had horses and land. I would go there for weekends and we would ride for miles over the moorland around Coniston Old Man. In the evenings we would shoot rabbits and enjoy Mrs Whitfield's wonderful cooking.

On Saturday nights, when there, we would get the bus to Coniston and go to the dance at the institute. We would blag drinks in the pubs and got really pissed. If the policeman came in they would hide me in the bogs until he left. To get back to Torver, we would walk along the railway line, perhaps 'stagger' would be a better description of our gait.

We kept a ferret at home called Rodney and we would use him to go netting. When netting, we would go to a rabbit warren, place nets over the rabbit holes secured with pegs, then put the ferrets down the holes. After a little while, the rabbits would bolt from their burrows into the nets, when we could catch them with ease. With luck, the ferret would appear a little while later.

Rodney was a big albino dog ferret, and Pete Aiery had a bitch who needed to be mated. They came to school and were placed in Philip's desk. This was during a history lesson. Miss Gottham, the teacher, asked, "What's that noise coming from your desk, Lockley?" "It's ferrets, Miss." "Well what are they doing in there?" "They're mating, Miss." "Remove them immediately," she said, and gave him detention.

How to prepare a rabbit. Take the unfortunate bunny from the net. Hold him upside down by the back legs. Strike him hard at the back of the head to break his neck (instant). Hold him with your left hand under his back, make a cut in the skin a the bottom of his rib cage, then cut to his groin, not too deep, or you will open up his guts. Then turn him over, belly down, and shake him vigorously, his guts will fall out, but you will need to free them from his arsehole, with a nick with a sharp knife. Then you must push your fingers into the rib cage where you will find his heart, lungs, and liver. To remove the skin, work your hand between his body and skin up and down his back, push the back legs back through the skin as far as you can then cut through the bottom of the legs, then pull the skin over his head and cut the head off at the neck. Bunny can now be jointed and ready for the pot. Bunny will not have died in vain, he would always make a good supper.

As soon as we started the Grammar School we joined the Scout Troop. I was in Shackleton Patrol. Earnest Shackleton has been my lifetime hero, so that suited me. We were about 50 in number, split amongst 6 Patrol's. Ted and Max were the masters who ran the outfit. They were good eggs and taught us a lot.

I always remember Easter Camp, it was in Lords Wood, a wooded hillside beside the Torver to Broughton road. We were transported there in a cattle wagon. On the way we would sing, "You'll never get to heaven in a Saunders Truck, cos a Saunders Truck is all to fuck," etc. etc. Fortunately, Mr Saunders hosed out the vehicle and put sawdust on the floor before our occupation.

Easter camp was to be endured. It was often cold and wet, some kids couldn't take it, and it was a bit embarrassing for their parents when they came to take them home, but most of us enjoyed it and took what we learned forward into our future lives.

CHAPTER 3

The Gondola

Father had some friends in Barrow who owned '*Gondola*.' She had been a beautiful steam launch, that had been owned by the Cavendish Family. It was said that Queen Victoria and Albert had sailed on her, but now she lay at anchor in Nibthwaite bay at the southern end of Coniston Water.

She had been converted into a houseboat with six double cabins amidships, a kitchen where the bridge had been and a bathroom replaced the engine room.

The forward saloon had not been touched and was still in its exquisite Victoriana condition. It was lit by gas, and at night was a fairy-tale place in which to be, we would play monopoly or a card game called Canasta, or just goof about. It was heaven.

We had *Gondola* for a month, each summer, during our early teen years. Dad had to go to work, so we would row him in the dingy to the old steamer pier on the west side of the lake at lake bank, where he would catch the bus to Barrow. Many years later, I was involved in rebuilding that pier, but that's another story.

Our friends, our parents' friends, their kids and pets would turn up. Cousin Leslie would be with us, the corgis, our Siamese cat Simon, and Twit the owl were there. It was heaven.

One day we were fishing for perch when Andrew caught a huge eel. He then killed it, opened it up, pulled out its liver and ate it! That was Andrew. Like when he found some rotten ducks eggs, which he hid on board.

We had been ashore, and were returning to *Gondola* when we came into Andrew's range. He lobbed the eggs, which landed in the dingy. As they exploded, they released a stench that you would not believe. There was no escape. Andy thought it funny, we did not.

Twit decided to fly ashore one day, but mistook a water lily pad to be dry land. She got quite a shock as she found herself breast deep in water. A rescue party soon picked her up only just in time, a near thing.

One day, I was running along the side of the boat, when I slipped and fell in. The water was about ten feet deep, I remember sitting on the bottom amongst the discharges from the toilet, I can still see the turds and toilet paper. I looked up and could see anxious faces peering down at me. At that point, I bobbed up to the surface. Dad said he would have jumped in, but had a ten bob note in his wallet.

Those weeks we spent on that boat were wonderful, swimming, sailing, and walking the fells, just like Swallows & Amazons.

Dear *Gondola* sank in the early seventies. She was rescued, restored by Vickers, relaunched and now plies up and down the lake. She is owned by the National Trust. Many years later, as a "grown-up," I was happy and proud to be involved in building her new slipway and jetty at Coniston.

Our school days were coming to an end, dad had a promotion, and was to open a new factory at Warsach, near Southampton. Beech Bank was sold, a great party was had, and we moved to a rented house in Grange-over-Sands.

It was here that poor Twit No.2 died (Phillip got her when we were shooting at Brackenbarrow). He gave her a mole to eat, she tried to swallow it whole. It was too big for her, so she choked to death. Very sad.

At this stage in our lives, we had to leave everything we had known and start a new life in the south. Phillip and I were fifteen. We were still children really, and for some time would miss the old life as we eased into the new one.

1 Mother knitting in the Gondola with Twit, Miffy and Minky
2 Miffy and Twit

CHAPTER 4

The Move South

The dye was cast, the furniture from Beech Bank had been put in store, we went to the leavers ball on the Friday. The car was loaded, dad, Phillip, me , the two corgis and Simon the Siamese cat, and whatever else could be stuffed into the old Austin 16. Mother went down by train, and we set off for Hamble, a lovely village on the Solent. Just south of Preston, one of the back wheels collapsed. She was an old car, and we were lucky to get there without further ado.

This was on the Saturday, no time for goodbyes. It was a bit sad really, I don't think that Phillip and I understood what a wrench it was until years later. We were still only fifteen. Andrew stayed in the north, he was working for West Cumberland Farmers in Whitehaven and was well settled.

On leaving, father said to Andrew, "You will be fine if you avoid the heavy drinking set." Andrew replied, "But dad, I am the heavy drinking set." (Prophetic.)

Having failed all our GCEs, much to the parents' disappointment, we'd elected not to go back to school. It wasn't that we were thick, we just wanted to go farming instead, and at fifteen, we were put to work.

1 Mother and father arriving into Mexico City
2 Queen Mary in New York taken by father
3 Mother and father with the captain of the Queen Mary and Sir Charles and Lady Dumphy

CHAPTER 5

The Farming Years

Father took us to the employment exchange. There we were found jobs; we were to work for the Frampton family. They ran two large farms at Netley and Hound. I worked at the Hound, Phillip at Netley. Both farms had dairy herds of about sixty cows each. One Jersey and one Friesian, both had large poultry units, and the hound had a pig fattening house, holding about one hundred pigs. They also grew a fair acreage of wheat and barley.

The herds were managed by cowmen Eric at the Hound, and Ginger at Netley. Phillip and I worked under them. So it was up at 4.45 every morning to be at work for 5.30 milking. Once I had loaded the churns onto the milk lorry, I would feed and muck out the pigs, collect the eggs and feed the hens in the deep litter houses. In the afternoons we would work in the fields preparing the land and planting the corn. Sixty cows make a lot of shit, as do a hundred pigs. So every day I would be scaling dung with the muck spreader, and with a tail-wind, much of the muck would land on me. Our land adjoined the Netley Military Mental Hospital, I would often spot escapees scuttling along the hedgerows. I carried a big stick on the tractor and would inform the hospital on my return to the farm.

We worked six days a week, doing the milking morning and afternoons, twelve hours a day under stern supervision, all for just over three pounds per week. One day, I remember weeping with exhaustion and frustration during a moment of reflection in the piggery. The pigs didn't give a fuck.

After about three months Phillip decided it was time to move on. He answered an advertisement in Farmers weekly from the Honey family who had a mixed farm in North Devon. George and Margaret Honey were dear people, they made Phillip a part of their family. He was very happy with them. Some weeks later, Phillip phoned me to say that Margaret's father had just acquired a farm near Holsworthy in the north west of the county and that he needed someone to work with him and his son Norman. Within a week, father whisked me down there in the old Austin 16.

I was introduced to the Colwill family, I followed 'Jack Colwill' and father as they walked around the farm, and discussed my future there. That was it, I was now in Devon, and father drove back to Hampshire. This suited the parents very much, as they were to move to Mexico because father became the Managing Director of Vickers de Mexico, a top job.

Stapleton Farm was in a state, Jack Colwill had sold his Farm in Heartland and acquired the place for £12,000, forty pounds per acre. The previous owners of the estate were the Rouse family, they had used the place as a ranch for many years, it was in a right state of disrepair and dereliction.

The farmyard was in the form of a quadrangle. A cottage, granary and shippon on the north side, cattle sheds on the east and south side, and buildings for machinery and tractors on the west. The lane to the farm was about a quarter of a mile long, and the farmhouse stood just below the yard on the southern side.

My first sight of the yard was of cattle, almost up to their bellies in dung, it was all a bit rough. There was little money to spend, so only the essentials were catered for.

Stapleton was a hill farm, and so qualified for the hill farm subsidy grant, supported in many ways. There was a lot of work to be done, Norman, me and Jack, who didn't like to do too much. He liked to go to the markets, and would generally come home pissed.

His wife, Alice, was known as mother, she was a Widdicombe before marriage, a real Devon name. She was a love, never stopped working, and was the prime person. We became very fond of each other. She was good to me. I think I had a crush on her, I was still only sixteen.

Stapleton was three hundred acres, we were a mixed farm, beef, sheep and barley. We had about twenty nurse cows who would suckle their own calves and another which we would buy in. We had to bring the cows in twice a day so that they could get used to the adoptive calf. All the calves were kept in at this time. This was my job: whilst the calves were sucking, I would milk the house cow, keeping an eye on the calves at the same time. We kept 200 ewes and four Suffolk tups. These the old man generally looked after.

The calves were weaned, then sold on as store cattle the next summer. That first spring, we ploughed and tilled eighty five acres of barley, under sown with ryegrass seed to provide pasture and silage after harvest. The drains and ditches had to be repaired for this, we got an old Priestman drag line ditcher. It was very old, but worked quite well. Some of the drains were six feet deep. The hedges and banks had been neglected for many years. Trees grew from the bank tops, so we spent days felling trees and laying hedges, and there were no gates, so we had eighty gate posts to set. These were produced from the oak trees we felled, as were the legs and purlins for the Dutch barn we built on the "Mow hay," (an area where the old hay ricks were built). To enable this we hired a steam-driven saw bench, which was massive. It was with us for a week, in which we produced eighty gate posts, and the sawn timber we needed to construct the Dutch barn, and the doors for the covered yard we were about to build.

How Norman and I managed to get through all the work we did, I will never know. We worked seven days a week, ten or twelve hours a day. I found it challenging and enjoyable, and for this I was earning six pounds a week as well as my keep.

So the routine of farming went on. Lambing, calving, ploughing and tilling, hay time, harvest, then preparing for winter.

That first harvest, we combined eighty five acres of barley. The corn was bagged directly on the combine, which was held on a chute and released at strategic points when necessary. These were to be picked up later that day and carried home to be dried and stored. Some were sold, and some we kept to be milled and turned into cattle feed, because we had our own mill and mixer. I really enjoyed the simple science of balancing the proteins, like linseed cake and brewers grain, and the carbohydrates from the rolled or ground barley for the livestock. We would add molasses to make the feed more palatable. Different recipes for different beasts.

CHAPTER 6

The Bull

Most of the cows we had were Red Devons, a well known breed of beef cattle. Our bull was of that breed, he was quite old and a bit grumpy. We never gave him a name. He would look at me with those dark menacing eyes, as if to say, "I'm going to have you one day."

One Sunday morning Jack asked me to go and check on the sheep. They were grazing along with the cattle in fields where we had not repaired the hedges. I noticed the bull standing in a gap, he was grumpy, pawing the ground, angrily growling, with his tongue hanging out. I decided to give him a wide berth as I went into the next field.

All of a sudden I heard thundering hooves and a loud bellowing. The old bastard was after me, full tilt. I set off of for the gate, as if I had wings on my heels. I vaulted that gate into the lane, I glanced behind to see him lift it from its hinges, and throw it into the air with his horns. I kept running, he kept coming, until I passed a field where some heifers were grazing. There was no gate to this field, so he lost interest in me and went to check out those young females.

The next bit of fun I had with him was when I went to feed him in his pen. The trough was in a corner and as I went to empty his rations, he pushed me, with his head and tried to pin me against the wall, but his horns were too long, so it gave me a chance to jump back over his head and out the door, pronto. He then lost interest in me and tucked into his feed. Feeling the hot breath of a 1 tonne beast just inches away, which could crush me to death, was a little unnerving, to say the least.

It was some weeks later, during harvest. In the long shed next to his pen, we would dry the grain. To do this we would build the sacks into a tunnel about thirty feel long, and six or seven feet high. Into this tunnel we would blow warm air, with a fan and heater designed for the job. It was very noisy and this must have pissed him off.

We had just completed the tunnel and were standing on its top. When we heard a bang and the next moment the old bull came into the shed, having knocked his door down. He was angry and started to demolish our stack with his horns, as we stood aloft, slowly sinking to the floor, as the grain spilled from the ruptured sacks. It was dark outside, Jack was in

A Red Devon bull. Now imagine him with horns and just inches from your face.

the yard and when he heard the commotion, he appeared at the entrance with a lantern. Having seen this, the bull turned and started to chase the boss up the yard. I have never seen Jack run before, but he was running now. The bull chased him out of the yard and up the lane where Jack ran into "little oaky field," the bull at his heels. Next thing was, Jack and his lantern, were hurled over the hedge back into the lane, fortunately unhurt apart from a few bruises and scrapes.

The old bull was sent to the slaughter house the next day.

The next bull we had was a Hereford. He was a doll and would let me ride him when we moved the herd to new rented pastures for the summer. We needed extra land for grazing, hay, and silage.

We had an extra hand by now: Ted Moore's. He had worked for the Honeys, but was on loan to us. One New Years Eve Ted and I were laying a hedge atop a bank. I was using the chain saw and was about to cut a branch, when Ted decided to point at that branch as I proceeded. Ted's finger was in the wrong place at the wrong time. His finger end disappeared with a little spray of blood. Poor Ted appeared at the pub some hours later, after spending some time at A&E, while we were all seeing in the new year. He bore me no malice, bless him, so I bought a pint.

Every year the parents would come back to England for a holiday. They always came by liner as mother would not fly, with them would come their car, this time it was a red Chevrolet, it had a red steering wheel, and in 1962 cut quite a picture in the Devon lanes. By now, the Honeys had moved to a farm near us, called "Halsdon Barton." It was a big farm, the ground was poor, but it was nice to have Phillip closer and the Honeys were kind to me also.

I must write about the winter of 1962, it was horrific, everything froze up, we had no water for eleven weeks.

Every day I would take a trailer to the stand pipe at the end of the lane, light a fire around it till the water came, then fill whatever vessels we could muster that would hold water. There was no water for bathing, so I didn't have a bath for eleven weeks. The animals were starving, and every day I would go around the farm to pick up dead sheep. I had to pluck the wool from them, then help the huntsman load the carcasses which were used to feed the hounds. The only way to get to the pub was by tractor, there would be two in the front bucket, one driving, and two standing in the transport box, as we drove through the bitter night. It was a tough time.

During the previous summer we had grubbed out a lot of hedges to make one huge field, it was nearly sixty acres, and in the middle of this expanse was a large building we called the sheep shed. It would provide some shelter for the flock and it was here that they were fed. Once the hedges had been removed, there were loads of stones left behind, which had to be picked up and taken away. Guess who got that job. Tedious back-breaking work that went on for weeks. Dear mother would come out and help me on some days, she could tell I was getting pissed off.

Back in winter now. The field was on an east-facing slope and on this particular day was receiving dreadful arctic winds and driving snow. I was taking a trailer load of silage to the shed, and as I entered the field I met the full force of the maelstrom. The tractor had no cab, and the blizzard was so strong, I could hardly see and the driving snow stung my cold face.

It was so cold it was impossible, so I made a plan so that I could get to the shed. I put the tractor into a low gear, aimed it in the direction of the shed, put a sack over my head and guessed how long it might be to get there, and set off. More by luck than judgement I was about fifty yards off target when I removed the sack. I was thankful, as I'm sure the sheep were, as I forked the steaming silage to them. It was from this field that I would pick up most of the poor dead beasts.

To warm up the feet when in the shippan (a cow shed), if I spotted a cow arching its back and about to piss, I would quickly get behind it and bathe my wellies in the warming torrent (bliss).

In the mornings we would have to light fires under the tractors to get them started, the oil became very thick and the diesel turned to slush in the injector pipes.

Spring came late and it was still cold for the time of year. We had sown barley in the big field, I was harrowing the grain in, but to keep warm, I tied lines to the steering wheel, set the tractor off, jumped off then ran behind the harrows, steering with the lines I had attached. I must have been quite fit then, but jumping back on was quite daunting.

Three hard years passed at the farm and, as the parents were living in Mexico City, Phillip and I had a month off at the end of 1963 to go and see them. Cousin Leslie picked us up at Paddington Station, took us to Millbank Tower, which was Vickers headquarters, where we picked up our tickets and visas etc. Then to Heathrow to catch our flight, which took us to Paris first, then changed to New York, and again onto Mexico City. As you can imagine, for two greenhorn 19-year-olds, this was quite an adventure, and also quite daunting.

Father was waiting for us, he had bribed the customs people, so we were whisked through with no problems.

Mexico was like nothing Phillip and I had ever experienced. It was a warm 25° every day, the air was filled with music and song, the people were gracious and father was seen as a VIP.

They lived in a beautiful house, just off Reforma, which had been previously the Swiss Embassy. There were two maids Angelina and Maria, and a house boy Tintin. This was luxury indeed.

The parents were now very well connected, with diplomats, rich Americans, politicians and even with the Army. One day we went out of town to the Army Riding School. I rode, but Phillip did not (until today). We were given two beautiful horses, and were schooled throughout the morning. By lunch time we were deemed competent to go off on our own. We rode through beautiful pine woods and upland meadows, sometimes at walking pace, a little trot now and then, building up to a canter. Phillip seemed to be coping quite well up till now, and was even grinning. We had been out for about an hour and a half when I decided it was time for home.

"Let's have a gallop" I said, and jabbed my heels into my stead. The horses knew they were going home and went like a pair of rockets. I looked back to see Phillip just hanging on for his life, and as we got to a little village, I had to pull up a bit to get round a corner. As Phillips horse slowed behind me, he half jumped, half fell off. His face was white, and he was panting hard. He called me a "fucking cunt," and would have hit me had I not been in the saddle.

Phillip declined to ride any further so he followed me back on foot, leading his bemused mount. That was the first and last time he went riding, ever!

Father was brilliant, he loved Mexico, and took delight in showing us the sights. Aztec temples by day, posh night clubs in the evenings, and on Saturday, the bull fights at the Plazza del Toros, a huge spectacle, everybody went to the bull fight.

After Christmas we went to Acapulco, staying over at Cuernaveca on the way, a beautiful place where film stars would often spend time.

Acapulco was fabulous, the sea was warm, everybody was chilled, and on New Years Eve, the place went mad, fireworks, guns being fired into the air (it seemed everybody had a

1 Father resting, Mexico
2 Mother's water colour of Miffy in the Mexico garden
3 Father in the same garden

33

1   Miffy and duck, Mexico
2   Father and mother relaxing sea
3   Young Mexican riders showing Phillip and I how it's done
4   The bull fight at the Paza del Toros, 1963

5   Mother in the garden with Alfonso, Mexico City
6   Mother swimming in the garden, Mexico
7   Mother at Tasco, Mexico

1   Mother, Phillip and myself on tour with our Chevrolet in Mexico
2   Father walking Miffy, Mexico
3   Mother tending to the birds in the garden, Mexico

gun). Mariachi bands playing everywhere, whilst mum and dad threw a party in our hotel, we felt like a couple of cool dudes.

On the way back to the city we stayed over in Tasco, an old silver mining town. This was old Mexico, all the locals seemed to be pissed on "Pulchi," a raw form of tequila, and the place had a feel of the old wild west about it.

Father took us to his office one day. It was in a skyscraper, and upon our arrival, dad had a pretend shootout with the car park attendant. I gather this was quite usual. He had four staff working for him, but on one wall, mother had painted a view of the Thames from Millbank Tower. It was brilliant and had made the papers when she completed it.

All too soon it was time to leave Mexico. We had a fabulous time, and it was thanks to the parents for having made it so.

Back on the farm again, early spring, and time to let the cattle and calves out to pasture. They are so funny, they go daft and get giddy. They run and jump around and make noises which must come from delight. I do think that animals have the capacity to be happy or sad.

Andrew was getting married to Sandra in Whitehaven. It was a bank holiday, Phillip and I hired a car and it took us fourteen hours to get to Cartmel. We slept in the car, and in the morning called in at the Airey's farm, where they gave us breakfast. Then on to Ulverston and to Aunt Margo's, where we were to stay that night. It was grand having a night out in Ulverston, meeting old friends and catching up with everybody.

The next morning, with a full English inside us courtesy of Aunt Margo, we set off for Whitehaven where we would meet Andrew to celebrate his stag night. He was on top form, and we had a great night with no mishaps.

The wedding was a grand family do. Aunt Alma, Aunt Margo, cousin Leslie and his girlfriend Margaret came. It was a shame our parents were not there, but of course they were in Mexico. In his speech, Andrew's best man Bill said to Sandra's parents, "Not only have you gained a son, but an alcoholic as well." (Prophetic.)

Things get a bit hazy after this, but I do remember driving back to Ulverston and then on to a party. We stayed with Aunt Margo that night (she had gone to bed long before we got in), but had prepared a sumptuous breakfast for us when we appeared in the morning.

Andrew was now working for Marchon Chemicals as a Technical Sales Rep., whose territory covered most of the south of England. He had rented a large flat in Malvern, so we all drove down together. There was a little cider house just five minutes from his place, so we got rip-roaring that night. With sore heads and light hearts, after having had such a lovely time, we set off for Devon.

I was becoming somewhat restless with the daily drudgery of life on the farm, I was thinking that there must be more that I could do in the future. The parents had been over and we had a family meeting on board a lovely transatlantic liner called the '*Oriana*' as she prepared to set sail across from Southampton.

I told father that I had been thinking of going to college. Father said I should talk to Uncle

John and ask for his advice, when Andrew chirped up saying that there was an agricultural college near him and that he would get in touch with them on my behalf. Sure enough, a prospectus arrived some days later and I was invited to go for an interview. That was it, I was in.

Hartpury County Farm Institute opened up a new world to me, we were about thirty students most were younger than me, but there were about ten of us who were over twenty, most of these were sons of tenant farmers from Lord Dulverton's Estate around Moreton in Marsh, they were great lads, and we all got along like a house on fire.

On entry to the college, my grant cheque arrived, whoopee, I thought free money. I purchased a Ford Popular car for fifty pounds, tailor made jacket and trousers, new shoes and two new shirts. Three days later a bill came for books and accommodation. This was a bit of a shock and I had to write to father to bail me out. He was very generous, and funding was provided forthwith.

On the second Saturday the local community kindly invited us to the harvest festival dance in the village hall. We all showed up, fresh from the pub and were made most welcome. As the dancing got under way, I noticed a very lovely girl, I plucked up courage and asked her if she would join me in the "gay Gordans." She said yes.

So off we danced. We got on really well and at the end of the evening I asked if I could give her a ring and maybe go out sometime. She said she would like that so I wrote the number down on a loaf of homemade bread I had bid for at the auction they held at the end of the evening, when the produce was sold off.

Janet was seventeen, I was twenty one, she had a beautiful voice with lovely soft skin. In fact, I met her 50 years later and found her to be as beautiful now as she was then. She was the youngest daughter of a farmer, whose farm was next to the college. It was a very large and prosperous place, so it was with great trepidation that I started to take her out. We were quite innocent and although I'm sure we loved each other, we never became lovers. Our relationship lasted through college and beyond, we were close and were great friends.

Life at Hartpury was great and, from being a lowly farm worker, I was starting to find my feed in the world. During the Christmas holidays, I stayed with Andrew and Sandra and got a job as a waiter at a local hotel. If we had a big function on I would recruit some of the Hartpury boys to help out. We had great fun and generally ended up very, very drunk.

I found the work at Hartpury pretty easy, as did my pals. We were that bit older, so had more farming and life experience.

One of my pals, Roger Holloway had a wet plucker, so just before Christmas we would kill and pluck chickens for the Christmas trade. We could process one thousand birds a day. I would kill them and Roger would pluck them. We were a good team, and some years later Roger became my best man.

As we broke up for Easter, I would take Janet up to Malvern in the old Ford Pop'. We went out for dinner with Andrew and Sandra, had a splendid evening, with plenty to drink, and then had to drive Janet back to Hartpury. Andrew had just acquired a Morris 1100, a company car. I persuaded him to let me take Janet home in that. Well off we set, me driving for too fast, and having had far too much to drink, managed to crash and write the car off. (The first of many).

We managed to get a lift back to Janet's where I stayed overnight, when Andrew came to pick me up the next morning he was most unhappy with me. I was most unhappy with myself and just wanted to crawl under a stone. It was cousin Leslie's wedding the next day. Phillip had come up from Devon with a girl in tow, and we were all five of us to go to Essex for the nuptials. We went out that night and all got very, very drunk. On our way home I tripped Phillip up for a laugh. He didn't see the funny side and proceeded to give me a good hiding, blacking my eye, and bursting my nose. I was quite shocked at his violence.

We got up early the next morning in order to get to the wedding, but before we left, Andy shot two Jackdaws, which had been on the lawn, and when a magpie came to investigate, he shot that too. We then bundled into a VW Beetle which replaced the 1100, it was a tight squeeze for five of us as we set off for London and the wedding.

Going along the north circular road we had the misfortune to bump into a car that had pulled up in front of us. The damage was slight, but we were delayed as names and addresses were exchanged. The girl from Devon proclaimed "I knew you shouldn't have shot that fucking magpie" (lovely girl).

We missed the wedding but got to the reception in time, which of course is the best bit. It was a weary journey back to Malvern that evening. Two days after this, I met Angus, a college friend and off we flew to Guernsey where his dad ran the electricity board.

They lived in a huge mansion, and we went there to work in the gardens. They were a lovely family, but Angus had a girlfriend who took a shine to me. Things became a little strained, so after a week, I flew home. I flew back to Heathrow and made my way to Uncle John's and Aunt Alma's house in Woodford Green. When I got there a garden party was going on. Mother was over from Mexico, she had come to sort Phillip out, he had acquired a double hernia and this needed fixing.

I had to get back to Hartpury as summer term was starting. Angus had forgiven me, my pals were here, so off to the Rising Sun we all went to catch up with each others adventures.

Some days later at around 2 o'clock in the afternoon I suddenly felt very ill, I had to go to bed and felt dreadful for 24 hours, it was some days later that I found out Phillip had gone to surgery at 2 o'clock on that day to have his hernias repaired (funny that).

Phillip returned to Mexico with mother for his convalescence. This lasted twelve months during which he had a gay old time. I think I missed out a bit there.

Another college friend was Jonathon Gooderham, his father, (the Major) had a dairy farm at Wickwar, near Chipping Sodbury. On alternate weekends we would go down there to milk the cows which enabled the herdsman to have some time off. The Gooderhams were very posh, but they liked me and made me very welcome there.

On Saturday nights John and I would go to Bristol and would get back to the farm very late and very pissed. It was on a Sunday morning we noticed that a wing chair that should have been in our bedroom was standing on the lawn in the sunshine. One of us had pissed on it the previous night. Who the culprit was we will never know, but things were a bit frosty over breakfast.

Another dear friend at Hartpury was Mike Minett. His family had a farm at Batsford, above Moreton in Marsh. He had a Ford Consul which he would lend me when I wanted to take Janet out. My old Ford Pop was out of commission at this point. I sold it for £5.

During that summer I went to the Three Counties Show at Malvern, where I demonstrated how to dress chickens and Turkeys. I felt quite important, especially as Janet's parents happened to see me in action.

I was very happy, I was liked and loved, I was now somebody, but not quite sure where I fitted in with the world. For me to feel at ease with myself would take some time. All too soon life at Hartpury was coming to an end. The exams had gone well for me but I had no idea what I wanted to do next.

Several weeks later, providence came to my rescue, and I was offered a job as a trainee manager with United Dairies in Moreton in Marsh.

1   Phillip and I as skinny teenagers

2   A fine example of a Priestman Tiger cub excavator, we used on the farm
3   Andrew and Sandra's wedding with me and Phillip, 1963
4   Twins at Andrew's wedding — not much meat on us
5   Leslie, Julian, Mother and Father at Norland Avenue, Barrow
6   Me at the United diary dealing with excesses of the spring milk flush

41

1   Winter 1963, coming over Dartmoor

2   A sheep farmer in winter conditions, similar to my normal winter day routine

CHAPTER 7

New Knee

Breaking into year 2020. I'm in my hospital bed having just got back from surgery for a brand new knee. They had provided me with an automatic knee-bending machine which did the work for me. The op' was a doddle, I had a spinal injection, with no sedation, so could chat to the surgeon and his team throughout the operation, quite an experience. During recovery, the exercises are bloody painful, but I was home in a couple of days.

It's funny how pain disrupts the creative juices, so after three weeks of no writing I'm about to return to my book…

…Back on the farm, the Minett family were tenant farmers who farmed at Batsford on Lord Dulverton's estate, close to Moreton in Marsh. It was there that I took lodgings, and so made Downs Farm my home. This was a classic Cotswold farm with honey coloured stone buildings which had stood the test of time. It was a big farm, so with a dairy herd, pigs and sheep together with acres of wheat, rapeseed and grassland, was a very busy place.

Mr and Mrs Minett were quite elderly but very active, so down to earth and such honestly good people. David ran the farm for his dad but also did quite a lot of contracting such as ploughing, bailing and combining. I would sometimes skive off work to help him during busy times.

Having settled in at the farm, I presented myself at the dairy in Moreton. It was a receiving depot for the milk produced around that part of the world. The milk was collected in churns, inspected and chilled, then sent to London in tankers. Part of my job was relief foreman on the plant. The foreman was called Sid, he was ex army, as were most of the men running that part of the depot. Sid hated the manager Mr Bowne. He would go into Mr Bowne's private bathroom and rub his private parts in Mr Bowne's personal fluffy cotton towel. An ex sergeant, he disliked authority as did most of the men on the milk deck. Imagine me, at 21 keeping these war veterans, mostly in their fifties, under some kind of control. Not easy.

Mr Partridge, ran the egg packing station there, so as trainee manager, I would cover his days off and holidays. The eggs were graded, packed, then sent out to stores and supermarkets up as far as Birmingham and Leicester. The packing station was staffed by girls, who were generally very cheeky, and would try to take advantage of my tender years. One, Dorothy, was giving me a hard time, so I threatened her with a good spanking. She persisted, so I grabbed her, put her over my knee, and tanned her arse in front of the whole depot. I got a good telling off for that part of my management technique. Imagine doing that today!!

Old Sam Borne was the farm inspector, so when he was off I would fill his shoes, so to speak, and go farm visiting to inspect and advise these "dyed-in-the-wool" farmers on their hygiene protocols, (milk can soon sour). Mostly the farmers thought I was talking shit.

I was Jack of all trades there, collecting churns, delivering eggs, driving the tankers to London, but one trip stands out in my memory. It was winter and had been snowing hard for several days so some farms could not be reached and were running out of churns in which to put the milk. Mr Bowne came to me in the afternoon and asked if I could take a lorry load of churns to Hook Norton where the farmers would collect them with their tractors. None of the drivers would go so I was happy to try. The lorry was loaded, the back wheels chained and off I set.

It was a bright, frosty night and the main road was clear but as I turned off for Hook Norton the snow got thicker and the drifts got deeper. It was not long before I was stuck fast, I left the lorry and walked to the nearest farm, about a mile, I guess. I was alone on this beautiful moonlit night. I was with foxes, badgers and owls as I stomped along and when I reached the farm, the farmer was only too happy to tow me out with his tractor. Off I set again, got stuck 2 more times, rescued again and finally reached the green in Hook Norton where the farmers were waiting for me. They were very happy, and my return journey was easy as I just drove in my own wheel tracks. I got home around midnight feeling very pleased with myself, but when I went to work the next morning, the shop steward said I had done a union man out of a job, I told him to go fuck himself.

My time at Downs farm and around Moreton was magical. Mike and I had a brilliant social life with young farmers. I was finding my feet at last. Mike and I were still only 21. He was keen on a girl he knew from Hartpury. She didn't feel the same, so that saddened him, I was still seeing Janet from time to time and she came up on the young farmers ball at the Lygon Arms Hotel in Broadway, a very posh affair and I felt so happy to be with her.

I purchased a lovely Riley 1.5 from Lady Dulverton, what a car. I was with Mike when we did my first one hundred miles an hour. It was along the straight at Snowshill, going toward Bourton on the Hill. He was such a great friend, and always generous towards me.

David let me keep a few piglets, generally the runts of the litters. I fed them on the reject eggs and milk from the dairy. They grew well on that diet, but it played havoc with their bowels, phew what a pong.

Phillip was still with the Honeys, who had moved to Cornwall to Gover Farm, which was in Mount Hawk, near St Agness on the north coast. Janet and I would take a holiday together, so off we set in the Riley bound for the coast. We stayed with the Honeys, but called in at Stapleton for the night on the way down. It gave Janet an idea of how I had lived beforehand.

The Honeys made us very welcome and we spent a lovely time just being together and living the moment. Phillip was the man about the village and was known as the young stallion from up Gover (I cannot imagine why)?

Janet drove part of the way back along the winding roads through the west country. She loved how fast the Riley would go. I had to gently remind her that 90mph was a little excessive as we neared Taunton. We talked of marriage, but over time our lives went in separate ways.

Mike was now working for BMC (British Motor Corporation) as a demonstrator on the new mini tractor they were producing.

We were now in mid-summer, the weather was glorious, and as I turned into the drive that led to the farm I noticed David was combining barley close by, but as I pulled into the farmyard, poor Mrs Minett came running from the house screaming "Mike's dead, Mike's dead."

My recollection of the next few minutes is a bit blurred. Mr Minett was milking in the parlour, I think I rushed there and told him to get to the house as soon as he could. I then jumped into the Riley and drove to where David was on the combine. He had nearly finished the field, so I climbed onto the harvester, he shot off to the farm in my car. It only took me about fifteen minutes to complete the piece and return to the farmyard where people had started to gather.

It was so awful, everyone was in total shock, but somehow we managed to finish the milking. I don't remember much about how. Mike was dead, how could this be? A hedge trimmer Mike was testing had a large circular saw blade fixed at the end of an arm at the rear of the tractor. The blade had shattered and a piece hit mike in the head, killing him instantly. Some went to the scene of the accident. I could not go, I was in total shock. I was desperate to cry but could not, I just felt so empty.

Later that evening, Mr Minett came to me and told me that the police would not let him go to Mike "if it was only to sit with him and hold his hand," he said. Mr Minett was a noble, beautiful man.

Some days later, Mr Minett came to my bedroom with a cup of tea. It was early and unusual. "Can you go to David," he said. "He's in the milking parlour and very upset." I got up and went to see him, he told me that Mike had been to see him, and to ask him to say that mum and dad were not to worry as he was okay and in a good place. He came to me some time later, or I think he did. My room was in the attic of the old farmhouse, I was in bed and woke up to feel a presence at the bedroom door. Instinctively I asked "Mike, what do you want." I pinched myself hard to make sure I was awake, I'm sure I was. The bed began to shake, the shaking became more violent. I was now holding on, when the bed started to levitate, 'honest', I was scared. The bed then settled when a cold, cold feeling started at my feet, moved up my petrified body, over my face and head, and was then gone. Did this really happen to me? Who knows? My mind is open, there are things of which we have little understanding.

Life moves on as it must, my work at the dairy became an easy routine, and I hope I was a help at Downs Farm. I was very happy in Gloucestershire, but was settling into a bit of a rut.

Mum and dad had returned to England from Mexico, and Phillip had gone back to Cornwall. Dad's office was in Millbank Tower, London and they had a flat in the same building. They came to Downs Farm one day to see me and to meet the Minetts. Father said to Mr Minett, "I hope my son has not been a trouble for you?" "Trouble?" said Mr Minett, "I don't know what we would have done without him." That pleased father, but made me feel very humble.

Summer passes into autumn and then to winter. I don't remember where I spent Christmas of 1967, but I do remember going carol singing with the young farmers, that was just too much, I was so happy and had so much fun.

In January, Unigate decided to send me to Eskdale outward bound school to do a management training course. It was to last a month and was said to be quite tough. So off to the doctor's for a medical, on the train up to London, to Liberty's, Piccadilly for boots and waterproofs, and then an evening with the parents on Millbank. The next morning saw me on the train from Euston to Ulverston. I stayed with dear Aunt Margo that night, after spending the evening catching up with old friends and visiting old haunts.

To get to Eskdale from Ulverston, I took the coastal line toward Carlisle. This line is exceptionally beautiful and follows the coast up to Workington before turning inland to Carlisle. I left the train at Ravenglass and was picked up by the school's lorry, then taken to Eskdale.

The Outward Bound School was built by Lord Rea in 1896 as a country retreat and was bought by the trust in 1950. An imposing building in landscaped grounds and with a tarn surrounded by woods. It was an ideal location as a base for our adventures during the next few weeks.

The ethos of the course was to instil self-reliance, confidence, and empathy, along with physical and mental fitness. Tough it was, half an hours circuit training followed by a dip in the tarn which was often ice covered, and all before breakfast. We were taught navigation, mountain craft and basic cooking, were taken rock climbing, shown how to use an ice axe, all in preparation for our final expedition which would come at the end of the course.

We were asked not to smoke or drink, although I had the odd fag. Our days were full, we never had a spare moment. We all had to give a talk to the rest of the community, my first attempt at public speaking, which I found a bit daunting.

One night we were loaded onto the lorry, dropped off individually, god knows where, told to make a bivvy for the night, cook breakfast, then find our own way back to the school, by use of map and compass. I had pitched my bivvy at a place called Drigg, with my shelter's back to the wind and settled down for the night. I was quite comfy until the wind moved 180° and it started to freeze. I was soon up, had some porridge and flapjack and was away not long after dawn. I remember it being a bright sunny morning, and my heart felt light as I walked the couple of hours it took me to get back.

The final scheme was a different matter. We would be away for three nights and four days. We had to climb as many of the 3,000-foot peaks as we could, and were not allowed to camp at an altitude of less than 1,800 feet. This was February, and it was fucking cold. We camped at Sprinkling Tarn on Scafell that first night. Some army people we met up there were going to do the same, but they chickened out and buggered off. "Too cold for us, lads," they said. In the morning everything was frozen solid — our boots, the tents, and even the primus stoves were reluctant to flare into life. Where we had slept, there were great indentations in the snow where we had melted it.

We came from Scafell via Esk Hause, onto Bow fell, then into Langdale and on to Grasmere. From there we went over Dunmail Raise to Thirlmere and started our ascent off Helvellyn. We climbed straight up from Wythburn Church and found ourselves in a white-out on very steep ground, cutting steps with our axes.

Some hours later, the weather had changed and it was now thawing and had started to rain. We were to camp above Thirlspot but found everything soaked, and the tents were leaking. We needed to think of an alternative. We dropped down to the main road to Keswick at Shoulthwaite and there I knocked on a farmers door. I explained our predicament. He told me he had just cleaned out a hen house and that we could use that for the night. I purchased two pints of milk from him, then marched down the field to our new home. The farmer had kindly given us two candles to illuminate our digs. With our sleeping bags rolled out, the candles lit, and the primus stoves roaring, this was five-star living compared with the alternatives. We had hot milky cocoa and flapjacks for supper that night. We were warm and happy as we fell asleep listening to the rain's assault on the hen house roof.

Being much refreshed, the next day we set off for Keswick and Skiddaw, but due to a shortage of time, we decided to go instead down Borrowdale to Great End, then skirting round the back of Wasdale screes, via Burnmoor Tarn and onward to the Outward Bound School. It had been a tough few days but incredibly rewarding.

I was sad to leave Eskdale, it had made a huge impression on me, and I was so fit that I could hardly stand still. I stayed with Aunt Margo that night and took the train to Euston on the next morning. I remember there being mini icebergs in Morecambe Bay as the ice on the lakes had started to melt and was carried to sea. I had arranged to see mum and dad at Millbank before returning to Gloucestershire and was happy to find Andrew there. He had just joined forces with a colleague from Marchon. Keith Simon, whose family owned a company called Amalgamated Laundries, and one branch of that company was Camille Simon Ltd.

Camille Simon made the laundry powders, detergents and bleaches to service the laundry group. Keith was the Managing Director and Andrew was the Sales Director. They planned to expand the business into the domestic and supermarket trade. I was invited to join them as Works Manager. This was a step up for me, a salary increase from £12 to £20 per week and the promise of a company car after the first year. Poor old Unigate, having spent all that money sending me to Outward Bound, were told that I would be leaving them for greener pastures.

Mum and dad had by now acquired a house in Windlesham in Surrey and although I was so very sad to say goodbye to the Cotswolds, I knew, deep down, that it was time to move on with my life.

It felt a bit strange moving in with the parents and adjustments had to be made on all sides. My drive to work was only about 30 minutes down the A30 to Chiswick. I remember well my first drive to work. I think it was the first week in April 1968 and the Cherry trees that lined the A30 were in beautiful blossom.

Carmille Simon Ltd was part of Amalgamated Laundries and the offices, laundry and the little factory stood behind a very imposing façade on the bank of the Thames at Strand on the Green. You can see it from the river as you approach Kew bridge from the east. A big Edwardian frontage which proclaimed "Pier House Laundry Ltd." I walked into a Victorian setup. The Simon family were known by their Christian names; Mr Dick, Mr Andrew, Mr Tom, etc. this did not suit me at all, but fortunately Keith Simon, my boss was of the next generation with a more modern outlook and with great ambition for the future of Camille Simon Ltd.

The factory came as a bit of a shock to me, the whole manufacturing plant, including cone-mixer and trough-mixer machines, had been squeezed into what had been a stable block. It was very dusty in there and George, who I suppose was the foreman, was covered in dust and wore a rag around his face rather than a proper mask. Raw materials were stacked everywhere and I wondered what I had let myself in for.

Our first big contract was with Sainsbury's. We made bath salts, floor and wall cleaner and pre-soak powder. The latter product contained an enzyme called Maxatase. This was pre-mixed with sodium sulphate and then added to the load. The dust from this stuff was lethal, and if you had a small cut, or an open wound in the morning, it would be much bigger by the end of the shift. It would attack the sweat on your face and make it very sore. We put up with some harsh conditions in those early days, it was not a very healthy environment in which to be working. We were so busy that improvements came slowly. In fact, as works manager I turned a few jobs down because of the harm it could have done to my staff. A line had to be drawn, people are not machines and will only stand so much before they kick back.

Although I was settling down in my new workplace, my heart was still in the Cotswolds, so most weekends I would head off there. Phillip had taken my old job at the dairy and was living near Chipping Campden, so it was nice to spend time with him and my old friends.

Things were getting very busy at Camille Simon. Andy was getting loads of new customers, I was taking on more staff, but we were just running out of space in which to operate. Andy and I became shareholders in the Company. We paid £50 each for our shares. I borrowed the money from dad, although I did pay him back. Eventually, my shareholding became

£40,000 when the company was taken over.

We were keen to find new premises, but prices were very high in and around London, so Andy decided that we come back up north to look for a place. We found a factory at Bardsea near Ulverston. It was built in the war, was 10,000 sq. ft. and we paid £10,000 for it, yes, £1 per square foot. This was at the end of 1968, a lot had happened to me in 12 months!

We moved the plant and stock to Bardsea at the beginning of 1969. Home again, who would have thought it.

While we were setting up the new factory we stayed at the Concle Inn at Rampside, near Barrow. The landlord was called Jim Barker, he had previously been a farmer and I had worked for him as a lad some 10 years earlier.

We were soon in production and moved to Ulverston. Andy and his family moved into a new house and I took digs in town. We were flying high. My company car came, I was now a director, the freehold in London was sold, it yielded Andy and I over £1000 each, big money in those days.

I became an eligible bachelor and enjoyed the company of quite a few girls. We were working hard, but playing hard too, life was good. I have to say how lucky we were to find the Bardsea factory. It stands behind a wood amongst fields and only 50 yards from the beach.

One Saturday Keith Simon and I had some work to do, we took a short break and walked to the shore. It was a lovely sunny morning, the tide was turning and sea bass were feeding on the flow, just yards from us. I said to Keith, "This is no job boss, this is a way of life." These were happy hopeful times!

It was at this point in my life that I met Margaret, my wife to be. A few of us went to Barrow for the evening, we were to meet some people in the "Tally Ho" Pub and once inside, someone said, "John, this is Margaret." Well, Margaret was a stunner. Red hair, white leather coat, a short mini skirt and white leather thigh boots, everybody was looking at her. I must humbly admit, that I was quite good looking too, so there was an immediate attraction and we started to hang out together.

I had been spending loads of money and found myself to be broke. Something had to be done. Sid Birt had the local Mr Softy ice cream franchise, that dear man let me loose with one of his vans and paid me 25% of what I took, it was Vickers holiday fortnight, the weather was lovely, so off to Walney Island I would go every morning to ring the chimes and sell my selection of ices. It was very hard work, but I made a lot of money in that fortnight.

Also, at this time, Brian and Doreen Davis helped me out. Doreen had a hair dressing salon in town. Brian was a jolly beer drinking rogue with a heart of gold. They took me in and I stayed with them for some time, free gratis. To these good people I will always be grateful. Margaret and I were now an item. Her mother, Peggy asked me what my intentions were? I answered "honourable Mrs Dixon," I was lying.

Mum and dad were about to go back to America again, this time to Chicago, so they came to Ulverston to meet Margaret and my future in laws. Dinner was a bit formal I remember,

1   Margaret happy at the allotments
2   Margaret looking beautiful our holiday in San Antonio, 1974

50

but Margaret's dad Harry, was a Vickers man too, he was a lovely chap, and I think my parents warmed to him.

Geoff Scott was the manager of an agricultural engineers, he lived in a fine house which belonged to his company. This house was to be sold at auction, and Geoff suggested that I should try to buy it. Off to the auction we went and I was the last bidder. £2,800 was the price, so I had to find £280 there and then. I had no money, but wrote a cheque, then rushed to the bank next door, told Riley Stubbins, the manager, who said, "No problem, John, we will cover it." I then went up the street to the Bradford and Bingley Building Society, said, "Can I have a mortgage, please?" Once again, "No problem, John." I was now on the housing ladder. Those were the days.

Margaret and I were now engaged, we had a house to move into and in June 1970 were married in the Parish Church where, years before, I had been a choir boy.

Phillip and Roger Holloway came up for the do, and on my stag night a crowd of us went to Barrow and the 99 club. I'm afraid we were asked to leave after a while, but we all had a fine time.

The morning of the wedding was warm and sunny, we boys all went swimming at Tridley Point at Plumpton, a well known bathing site on the estuary and then to get spruced up and off to the Pub. I had booked the church for 3 o'clock (pubs closed at 3). We all rolled up in fine form. Roger was my best man, Margaret turned up just a little late and all in all the wedding went without a hitch. However, as we were having our photographs taken outside the church, Andrew set off two distress flares. There was red smoke everywhere and some thought it a joke in bad taste. We had the reception in the Sun Hotel, it was a grand affair, everybody had a good time, and to round off the evening Derek and Eleanor Wild threw a party for us at their house. Derek brewed his own beer, it was very strong, and saw one or two out of the game.

We all got back to the Sun around midnight and as one would expect, our bed was full of all sorts of junk, at least, no grass snakes.

We were to honeymoon on Jersey and drove down to Moreton in Marsh the next day. We stayed at the Manor Hotel that night, a posh treat. We took the ferry from Weymouth the next day and landed on Jersey where a little Triumph Spitfire was waiting for us. Margaret's friend, Sue worked for Hertz rent a car, and she had arranged it. Those were good times.

We came home and settled into married life, generally we got on fine, but Andrew and Phillip were around and we were like the three Musketeers, often going on the beer, partying and getting home late.

The house had a bay window. Growing beside this was a Virginia creeper which I could climb and gain entrance through the bedroom window above, as Margaret sometimes locked me out.

Andrew and I went to Edinburgh to see a supplier. These were always boozy affairs, it seemed to be the corporate norm in those days. As we were returning, heading south, near

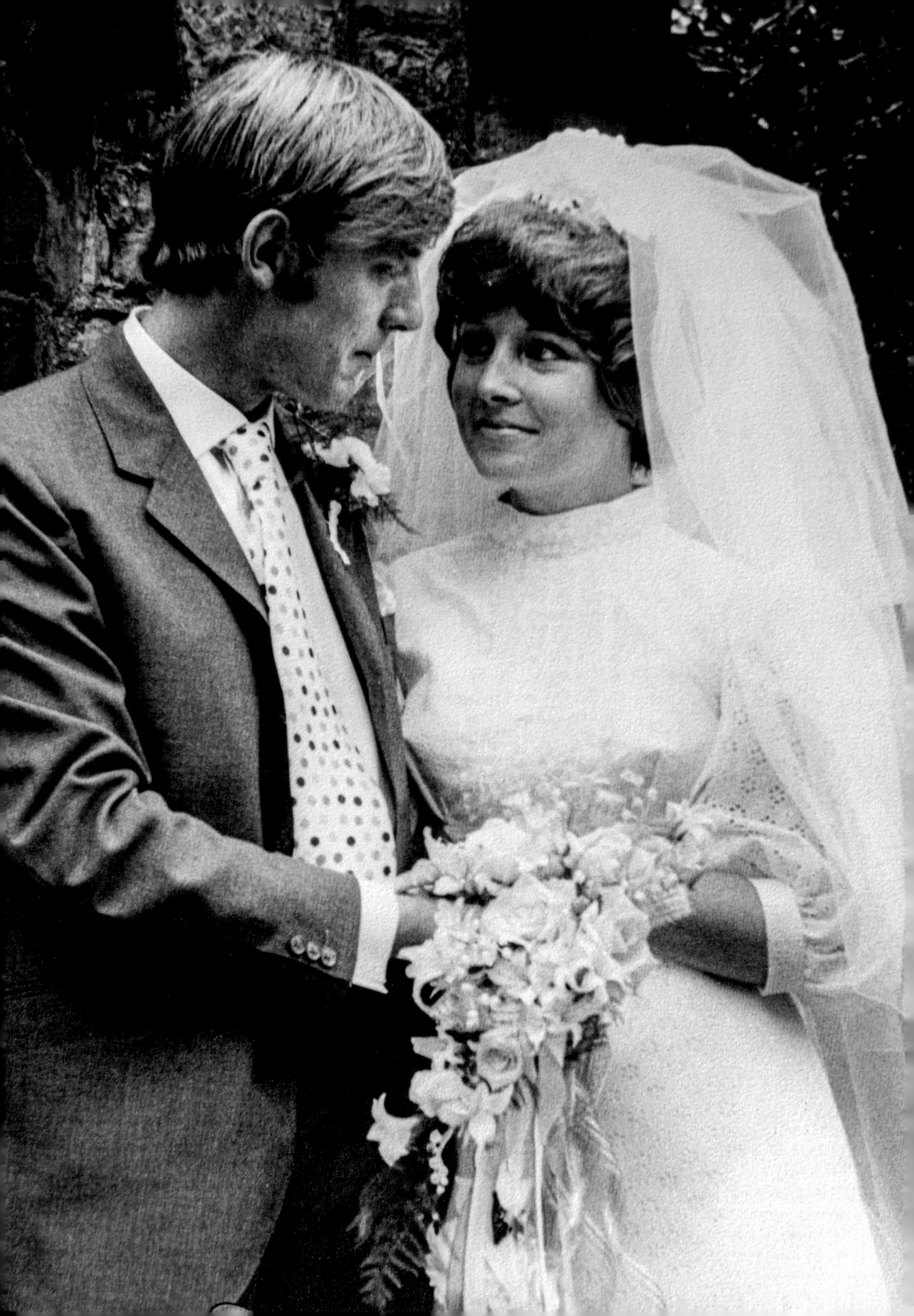

<   Our wedding and loving gaze
1   Margaret on our honeymoon
2   Our wedding day, June 13th 1970
3   Me at the beach in Jersey on our honeymoon

Carlisle Andrew suddenly grabbed my arm "Johntie," he said "I've got a horrible feeling of impending doom." I just thought it was alcoholic remorse.

Having dropped me off at my place he went home, it was around 6 o'clock in the evening. Two hours later, Andrew returned, distraught and in tears. "Dad's dead, dad's dead," he wailed. I felt little emotion and was more concerned for Andrew. I took him to the pub, we had a couple of drinks, then went to see an old friend of my parents, Barry Charles. Barry had been a submarine commander in the war. I knew he would be good in a situation like this. His counsel was always measured and pragmatic. We opened a bottle of champagne and drank to the memory of Father, and then opened another. We stayed with Barry that night.

At work the next morning we managed to get hold of mother. Andy broke down when on the phone, he was like a child, crying "Mummy, mummy." I was quite disturbed by this. Dad had some business in Mexico City and had been driving down from Chicago as mother would not fly. They got to Fort Lauderdale, where dad had had enough of driving and persuaded mum to fly the rest of the way. They stayed over that night and were having a nightcap on the veranda when father slipped and bruised his chest. This proved to be fatal.

The next day they flew to Mexico and booked into the Hotel Geneve. On the following morning dad got up and complained of an indigestion. As he started to shave, a thrombosis struck and killed him instantly. This was so sad. Dad was only 58 and was at the top of his game. His mortal remains still rest in Mexico City.

Andrew was tasked to escort mother back from Chicago, I was worried for his mental well-being, he seemed to be drinking more and more and the control that dad somehow had over him seemed to be slipping away.

Mother went to stay with Aunt Alma on her return and Andrew returned to work. He was angry and blamed mother for dad's death. I know this was irrational, but he had made up his mind.

Margaret and I had been married for about 6 months when mother phoned and asked me to go to Essex to fetch her as she had decided to come and stay with us. I was so busy with work that I could not spare the time. I told her that Alma would pop her on the train at Euston and I would pick her up at Ulverston Station. This did not suit, mother calling me an "ignorant selfish little shit."

The next day she turned up in a black cab at a cost of £200, a great deal of money in those days. Mother was a very difficult person. She was an alcoholic, selfish and quite demanding. This put quite a strain on our marriage. She was lonely and would want to come out with us to parties and gigs, where she would get pissed and make a fool of herself. Her old friends were shy of asking her round, they couldn't afford the whiskey. One day she said to Margaret, "I'm his mother and I come first." That just went down like a lead balloon. It was some weeks later when she cooked an ox's heart for dinner. It looked most unappetising and I declined to eat any, this made her angry so she called me "a little shit" and continued, "I'm checking out of this place." She left and booked in at the Sun Hotel.

Within a few weeks she had got herself a little house near the town centre. It was dark and horrid, I had tried to talk her out of it but she reminded me of my "shitty ignorance."

We had now expanded and took a 26,000 sq. ft. factory in Barrow. At this point we were employing about 70 people. Andrew was becoming more unstable. He would call in at the Bardsea factory to see me in the mornings, whilst on his way to Barrow. He would open his briefcase which had within it a bottle of whiskey, "Have a drink with your old brother," he would say and off he would go. By mid-afternoon he would be roaring drunk. Somehow he managed to keep his position, but it was becoming increasingly difficult for me to manage. He became quite grandiose, like when he spent a fortune on a Christmas party for the management one year. He would have work done on his house, and charge it to the firm. Any work by outside contractors would be secured by giving Andy a percentage of the cost. I found this difficult to live with.

He purchased a lovely fishing boat in Holyhead, the *Odin*. We went down to sail her back to Barrow. Fortunately the weather was good and — more by luck than good judgement — we found our home port after 16 hours at sea. He actually employed a friend to look after the boat, once again on the company.

When sober, Andy was a top chap, but his drinking bouts became more and more regular. One day the Sun Hotel rang me in a panic. Andrew was sitting in the cocktail bar with a Luger Pistol in hand, and a bandolier of bullets round his neck. I managed to get the gun from him, and we put it in the hotel safe. The next morning he retrieved it and turned up at the Bardsea Factory, gun and bullets ready to go. We were having target practice with it when the police arrived in a panda car. That was the end of the Luger, and Andy was fined £40. After he was fined, Sandra said "Oh, how dare they, and a man in Andrew's position too."

I had sold the house in Lightburn road and purchased a converted barn at Plumpton Hall, it was about 50 yards from the beach but was unfinished, so we moved in with Margaret's parents. They were nice people, but lived in a different world to Margaret and me. Margaret and I had a rather unstable marriage, the pair of us having embarked on affairs and at one point having moved to Plumpton, I left her for a while.

Mother was in hospital drying out, so I moved into her flat. These were strange times, I was working very hard, had a manic social life and was drinking a lot as well as taking Valium. Andrew had now left Camille Simon and had moved with his family down to Cornwall. They had fallen on hard times, Andy was often drunk and when sober would sometimes go into a fit. It was so sad, they were now on benefits and lived in rented accommodation in St Agnes. Andy called the social security man, the man with the golden hands. Drink had taken everything from him, but for the life of him, he couldn't stop. When he did try, he left his family in Cornwall and returned to Ulverston to stay with mother. At this point I have moved back in at Plumpton. It was an upside down house, the garage, bedrooms and bathroom being downstairs and the kitchen and dining area upstairs, and on another level was a huge living space. It was a great place for parties, and we entertained a lot. Poor Andrew was still drunk most of the time, and his health was suffering badly.

Andrew was in a bad way by now, so dear Aunt Margo found him a place at a hostel/clinic run by the church in Newcastle upon Tyne. She made lunch to bid Andy bon voyage, there were about 8 of us present and Andy, true to form, turned up drunk with a half empty whiskey bottle in his hand. "I'm fucking pissed again" he said to Margo, who replied that she had been around for too long to let anything Andy might say to shock her. That lunch was the last time I saw Andy alive.

Andy died three days later at the hostel. They had no drugs to treat his condition, so he took a fit, swallowed his vomit and drowned. I had to go to the hospital to identify poor Andy, who was finally at peace, and then on to the inquest. I was angry with the people who ran the place, but they were devastated by what had happened, so I decided not to kick up a fuss. I don't think Andy would have ever conquered his love-hate relationship with the bottle.

Mother never came to Andy's funeral, she stayed in bed with a bottle of scotch and a box of chocolates. This had been her coping strategy ever since we were kids.

Mike Tullis. Photo: Paul Renaulf

Sandra and the boys scattered Andy's ashes on High Peel Near, an isthmus on the east side of Coniston water. I must say that I had little to do with Sandra until she asked if I would like to buy Andrews shares in Camille Simon. I thought, why not. So I paid her £500, ten times what he had paid for them. I thought this was a fair offer. This was confirmed by Eric Edwards who was an okay chap and our new Managing Director, who had been hired to take the company toward a takeover. I did not know at that time that was his role.

Mike Tullis was an engineer and contractor, we hired him to build a new warehouse and to extend the loading and outdoor storage areas. This kind of work interested me, so when he was busy, I would take a couple of days off work to give him a hand. I learned how to drive excavators, how to use explosives, and we became good friends. He had a 28' Sloop, "Salone," on which he had done lots of modifications. She was a fine craft, moored at Roe island near Barrow. We would sail up the west coast of Scotland, round the Isle of Man and from time to time Margaret would join us, but the sailing life didn't suit her, so my girlfriends would come instead. I was his best man when he married Liz and would work for him some time later. You will read of this later in the book.

With us having built new warehousing, we had some extra storage space. Mike Conlong was a haulage contractor who was shipping goods by lorry to the Middle East, so we would collate the loads and despatch them when ready. He was quite a character who had contacts in Europe and beyond. Margaret became his secretary, and it was decided that we should drive an old Land Rover down to Doha in Qatar, meeting agents on the way down. I was hoping to drum up some business for Camille Simon from that part of the world, so off we set on an adventure through Europe and the Middle East.

Mike and Steve flew to Belgrade, Roger, who was to be the mechanic on the trip and I were to take the ferry from Hull to Rotterdam and meet them in Belgrade at the National Hotel. We missed the night ferry and had to wait for the morning sailing on the next day. Having lost 12 valuable hours we made best speed south, which wasn't easy in the old Land Rover, even though she had a "Fairey" overdrive. I found that if I got close behind a lorry, I could get a tow from the vortex it created. This was demanding driving and not much fun. By midnight we had reached Saltsburg, managed to get some supper, then grabbed a few hours sleep in the back of the Land Rover.

We set off for Belgrade, via Zagreb that morning. At the border posts, Roger would ask, "Me Wantum stampum on passport." I thought, daft bugger. Well, the drive down to Belgrade was a nightmare, the road was narrow and rammed with traffic heading south. There were wrecked vehicles all over the place, some on fire and some with their loads spewed over the ground. The only information I had was that we were to meet at the National Hotel. Where that was, I had no idea. It was a horrendous journey and was getting dark as we approached Belgrade, when by good luck, I spotted a sign: National Hotel. We arrived at that place half an hour behind the other two. That had been some drive.

After a fine supper and a good night's sleep, we four set off, heading south. This was 1978 and at this time Yugoslavia was a beautiful settled country. We found a hotel that night, and it was a bit rustic to say the least, but interesting. On the next day, we crossed into Bulgaria. This was an eye-opener, like stepping back one hundred years. We had to swap our currency for tokens, the food was shit, but the scenery was stunning. I remember driving through a town called Plovdiv, just before we crossed the border into Turkey.

South to the Bosporus, over the new bridge and into Istanbul. This city had everything, it was exotic, frantic, beautiful, and disturbing at the same time. We found a hotel and it was here that I found out that Mike had been having an affair with Roger's wife. This randy bugger decided to fly back to England to spend a naughty weekend with her. We were to continue south, and he would meet us in Damascus. This caused a problem: the Land Rover was on Mike's passport so could not be taken from the country without him. It had to be transferred to mine. This entailed trailing around government offices, costing a great deal in bribes and took a whole day. We were a bit pissed off, but said nothing. Poor Roger thought he had to go back for some urgent business, not having a clue about the real reason.

We dropped Mike off at the airport and headed off to Syria. Driving down through Turkey was a wonder, mile after mile of open grassland, with quaint wooden habitations from time to time, over the beautiful Taurus Mountains, then down to Mercin, on the gulf of Iskenderum. We stayed here in this lovely seaside town for a couple of days when Margaret, who was Mike's secretary, sent us a Telex informing us that Mike was having a struggle getting a return flight (dirty bugger).

The countryside in this part of the world was stunning, we were so lucky to be able to make this journey. From Turkey, we passed into Syria. A small problem with the Land Rover insurance was soon sorted with a bribe of £20. On we drove through this beautiful country until we came to a pretty town called Hama. We found lodgings and also found we had run out of money, it being the evening so the banks were closed. We were sat on our balcony overlooking a large square, when two guys appeared on the balcony next to us. After chatting with them they told us not to worry about money as they would stand dinner. This meal was one of the most memorable interludes of my life. The little restaurant sat on the river bank under a huge Roman aqueduct. A water wheel was creaking and groaning its way round. It must have been fifty or sixty feet high and a thousand years old. For our repast we had carp, salad, hot fresh bread and Syrian beer, just delicious and the gay couple paid. They were really nice guys and cracking company.

When we got back to our hotel, we were surprised to find all the corridors occupied by sleeping Arabs, we had to step over them to get to our room. Evidently this was quite normal. After getting some cash the next morning, we set off towards Damascus. Syria was then a beautiful country. It is an absolute crime that it has fallen into the hell hole it is now. We came to Damascus and found a hotel overlooking one of the main squares in the centre of the city. In this square people were publicly hanged, we were told, fortunately not on this particular week.

Mike was still struggling to get a flight, so we had three days in the city. Damascus is a mind blowing conflict, modern and ancient with evidence of British Imperialism still present in many of the buildings. Walk a few yards from a modern shopping arcade, and you would find, by the river, sheep and goats being slaughtered on the bank. The unwanted offal being tossed into the flow, and the sandy bank red with blood of the poor, now dead beasts. As they say, man cannot live by bread alone.

Mike finally got a flight, so off to the airport we would go. At that time things were starting to go wrong in Lebanon. All the way to the airport, tanks and field guns were dug in beside the road with their nasty bits pointing west. We were going south.

The atmosphere at the airport was a little strained. We boys were a bit brassed off having hung around for three days, but Mike, being his ebullient self, lifted our spirits as we headed for the Saudi border. Funny thing: there was no border, we just went along the Baghdad road, then swung a right into the desert. This was known as the Tap, a series of tracks across the sandy waste, with just the occasional oil drum to mark the way. After a few hours, we came over a dune to be confronted by a huge fort, and from this fort came racing towards us a Toyota pick-up truck with a machine gun mounted in the back. Three guys dressed in white robes stepped from the vehicle and strode towards us, "Customs." They searched the old Land Rover from top to bottom, patted us down, as the police here do, went through our passports and papers, then one said to me, "You speak any Arabic?" I replied in the negative. He responded, "Then you should bloody well learn," and I replied, "Yes sir, I will start tomorrow."

They were okay and we were waved on our way through the desert. Four of us sleeping in the Land Rover was a pain. We drew lots as to who would sleep where, one in the front, one in the middle and two in the back on top of everything. Most uncomfortable, but needs must. We came to Whadi Huf Huf, (the name stuck in my mind). There we were able to have a shower, a shit, and a shave. All a bit basic, but that's what adventuring's all about. After a simple meal, we headed once again into the great unknown. Finally, we came to a Whadi which we guessed was the border between Abu Dhabi and the Emirates. A Danish guy was washing his lorry by the little pond, and he invited us to join him for a beer. This was most unusual and, had we been caught with alcohol, we would have been heavily punished. Nevertheless, he produced the contraband from a secret chilled compartment in his cab. We spent a very pleasant hour with this stranger, forbidden fruits always being the sweetest. As we left the Whadi, we found ourselves on a proper road again, and taking a right turn at a crossroads found ourselves in Abu Dhabi, and in no-man's-land between customs posts.

Somehow we managed to backtrack and finally arrived at the Qatar boarder where Roger had a bit of a problem. As he had a Canadian passport, he needed a visa to gain entry, so we had to leave the poor soul at the border as we proceeded to Doha. Fortunately, Roger was allowed to join us at our hotel, but under the promise that he would stay with us and fly out the next day. Here, I met a Lebanese guy called Jack Sousou, he had connections with the royal family there. We talked of my business, and considered the possibility of starting a factory there producing detergent powders which could be sold and distributed throughout the Emirates. This project seemed very promising, but several weeks later and it came to nothing.

Having stayed in Doha for a couple of days, we managed to sell the Land Rover, said our farewells and flew home.

Whilst we were away, Margaret had spotted a house she liked, so she put in a bid which was accepted. We had not been happy at Plumpton, so having sold that for a good profit, found ourselves to be the new owners of Willowdene Gardens.

Work was becoming a chore — the more we grew, the more departmental we became. I was having to deal with people who didn't always agree with me, and I found this quite frustrating. I was still having lots of fun though. Dave Shaw had a pub, The Globe, in town and I would help him behind the bar sometimes. He was a great character who also had a fishing boat, the *Derry Jeane.* I would crew for him when we took parties of fishermen out for the day. One time we hired a lovely 34-foot sloop at Inverkipp and had a week's sailing on the west coast of Scotland. Peter Seeds, who also had a pub in town, The Hope and Anchor, an ex-Fleet Street journalist was with us on this trip. These boys were such fun and such good friends to me.

If not out with the fishing, on Sunday mornings I would play golf at Bardsea with Geoff Scott and some of his farming friends. Geoff had started his own company as a machinery dealer. So in those early days, I would go and help him out, buying and selling all sorts of farming gear, from milking machines to tractors. All of these things I was involved with, as well as being in the Round Table, having a hectic social life and keeping my end up at the factory.

Margaret and I were getting along. At this point, she had been on the pill for ten years and was advised to stop, and around Christmas, New Year of 1979, Becky, our beautiful daughter was conceived. We really were getting along well.

Bruce Ellery was the landlord of the Farmers Arms in the town centre and he was entertaining Tim Hartley, the M D of Hartley's Brewery one afternoon. Tim complained of being cold, as they sat around the fire. Bruce, who had a tarmac business, went out back to get some paraffin to liven up the fire. What he thought was paraffin was petrol, and that was how he burned the pub down.

Some days later, Dave from the Globe got a team together to play Ambleside Rugby Club. Bruce and I went along with others to support them. Bruce's burnt hand was heavily bandaged and he was feeling a bit sorry for himself. After watching the game for about ten minutes, Bruce was feeling like a beer. "Let's go up to the Golden Rule." He knew the landlord and his wife, Dave and Ann Oldham. We were at the bar talking with our hosts, when Bruce lit up a cigarette, resulting in him setting fire to his bandages. He looked so funny and bewildered as he tried to extinguish his flaming hand. It was the first time I had been in the Golden Rule, little did I know that it would play such a huge part in my future life.

As spring moved into summer Margaret's tummy expanded with Becky. I had never seen her happier, or more contented, pregnancy suited her. My job with Camille Simon was still very demanding but meditation at the Manjuschri Buddhist Institute at Conishead Priory, near Bardsea, twice a week, helped a lot. The priory, is well worth a visit, a fine place run by fine people. Prior to being a monastery it had been a convalescent home for the Durham miners.

In the beginning of September I had a strangulated hernia which needed urgent surgery, and as I recovered from the operation, Becky was born. As I was not able to drive, Margaret went to Barrow by ambulance, I showed up the next day to meet my new beautiful daughter and as I walked by the Market Cross, the town crier was announcing the Millennium Anniversary of Ulverston's Town Charter. I took advantage of this situation and got him to announce Becky's arrival to the gathered crowd.

Margaret and Becky came back to the hospital in Ulverston the next day and on the evening after I was summoned to go and fetch them home. I was to take some mother and baby things with me, but what I thought was suitable, was not suitable!! I had been drinking with Tim Hartley and Dave Shaw, and was somewhat inebriated when I showed up, as Margaret and the ward sister berated me. That took the daft grin off my face, and I was asked to go away and not to return until sober.

Becky was an easy baby, she was placid, happy and slept well at night. We were settled as a family and spent Christmas and New Year quietly with friends and what family we had around us. Mother was still around, and had moved into a flat on Church Walk, quite near Aunt Margo.

Alma came to visit her and mother decided to dye the living room carpet brown. Whilst her carpet was drying, they came to visit us at Willowdene. Our carpets were a pale fawn colour and mother's shoes, still damp from her carpet, transferred some wonderful brown footprints across our lounge. This made Margaret so happy, (not). Poor mother was so embarrassed, that we had to ply her with a very large whisky. Alma was very concerned for mother's health, so she decided to take her back to London with her. This would only be for a short period, as Uncle John could only take mother in small doses. He had once said to Margaret, "Please don't bring Phyllis here any more."

One Monday morning in March I was in the office when I answered the phone. It was Dave Shaw who asked if I would speak to Tim Hartley. I was so surprised when he asked me if I would like to take the tenancy of the Golden Rule in Ambleside. The thought of being a publican had never entered my head, so I asked Tim how many days would I have to think about it, he told me "three." I knew that the pub was a good one, but would have to give up the life I had known for the previous 15 years. Twas a great dilemma, then I thought that if I didn't try, I would never know.

Forty years on, I knew that I had made the right decision.

CHAPTER 8

The Golden Rule

When the time came for me to leave Camille Simon, I was ready. I had no idea what lay ahead of me. I had given up my security for what was to become a lifetime of adventure.

April 9th 1981, Lockley became a publican. When I got to the 'Rule,' the place was a hive of activity. Stock takers, valuers, the delivery lads were delivering my stock, the brewery big wigs were there with my tenancy agreement for me to sign, then off I went to the magistrate's in Windermere to get my license. By midday the pub was mine, and the bar was open.

I had one week to prepare myself for the storm that was about to hit me. Easter week, when Ambleside transformed from being a sleepy country town to a hotbed of tourists and visitors. Gangs of Hells Angels came, groups of fell walkers arrived by the thousand, casual trippers would fill the streets looking for sustenance and somewhere to set down with a cup of tea and a bun.

On the Good Friday morning, there was a queue, about 50 yards long, of people waiting for opening time. As I opened the door, they surged forward. Some of them looked really rough and I suspected were already inebriated, so I had to stand at the door to select who my customers might be. The rejected ones were most unhappy and called me names as they skulked off to find an establishment which would admit them. There were such places, so fights and drunken brawls, which spilled out onto the street, were common. Broken Newcastle Brown bottles littered the street as rival gangs hurled them at each other. It was a baptism of fire for me, but the weekend went without incident at the Rule. I was lucky. I had inherited a good staff from the Oldhams and they were a great help to me that Easter weekend.

The Friday and Saturday were crazy but things started to settle by Sunday, and although very, very busy, became more manageable. People had started to go home on Easter Monday, so things calmed down a bit, as the traditional visitors got into their holiday routine.

I could not believe how busy we had been on that first Easter week. We sold 23 x 36-gallon barrels of Hartley's best bitter, that's around 6,600 pints. That's a lot of beer, I thought, I'm gonna be rich.

1 Picture of the Golden Rule backyard in 1948, given to me by John Elleray who was then the landlord.

2   Me working the camera at my first day at the pub, April 1981. Photo: Mike Barker
3   Me celebrating my first day at the pub. Photo: Mike Barker

The staff were very professional. I remember Phil and Veronica, Caroline and Beverly who were both students of Charlotte Mason College. There was Mrs Etchell the housekeeper, she was a dear old girl, but couldn't manage the change of regime, so we parted on good terms.

We had kept the house in Ulverston, and as Becky was only six months old, she and Margaret would spend three of four days a week away from the pub. The brakes were off, so the landlord, who was working hard, started to play hard too.

For the first eighteen months at the pub I was seldom sober. Mother was still alive, so I would visit her in her little flat in Ulverston. She loved her whiskey and was taking Valium as well. I took advantage of her hospitality by downing both. This would set me up for the day.

I didn't realise this at the time, but my life had started to run out of control. I was becoming big headed, Jack the Lad! I was chasing women, staying out all night, and must have been a pain in the arse. I thought I was doing great.

The pub was doing very well, and although pissed, I could hide it so people would visit to enjoy the "bonhomie" that was to be had at the Rule.

So much was happening during this time that I'm finding it hard to elucidate. Some of my customers were rock climbers, some students, but two — Tony Greenbank and Ian Wall — were professional guides. It was not long before Ian had me on the end of a rope, and I remember that the first climb we did was overhanging Bastion on Castle Rock, a Lakeland classic. Ian was Veronica's estranged husband, he now works in the Himalayas. Tony Greenbank was an author and journalist, an ex-librarian, he loved climbing, was a member of the Fell and Rock Club, and had been an Outward Bound instructor. He was a huge character and was known by the locals as "Clout." A local term for dish-cloth, which was Cumbrian irony, as Tony was so wonderfully intelligent and articulate.

The first time I went out with Tony was when we went to climb the "New West" route on Pillar Rock in Ennerdale. To get there we first drove to Wasdale Head, we then walked up Black Sail Pass, over the ridge into Ennerdale, along the Climbers Traverse and thence to Pillar Rock. I found the trek exhausting. But Tony spurred me on. "Hey man," he would shout from fifty yards above and ahead of me, "you're doing great, not far now, man."

Pillar Rock is big — very big — and I thought 'what the fuck am I doing here' as we got to the base of the climb. We put on our rock shoes, roped up, and Tony set off up the first pitch. This was a long run out, and I could barely hear him when he shouted that he had reached the first belay. I was nervous, so decided to take a Valium. The rope was taken in, and I heard a faint "Climb when you're ready." "Hang on," shouted I. "What?" shouted Tony. "I'm taking a pill." "A pill, what pill?" "A Valium." I heard a "Fuck me," and the rope was pulled tighter. "Climbing," shouted I, as upward I went, feeling a little more relaxed.

One could not have had a better climbing partner than Tony, he was always positive and full of encouragement. At the top of the climb, we had to abseil into Jordan Gap in order to walk off to Dawhead screes into Wasdale.

At the head of Dawhead Screes we sat down and Tony was surprised when I produced

1   Me climbing New West on Pillar, on another wet day
2   Same route
3   Tony Greenbank climbing behind me on New West, led by Bill Birkett who took the photo for a book he was writing
4   The irrepressible Tony Greenbank at home on the mountain

four cans of beer. Surprised but delighted. Feeling much refreshed we ran down that scree and back to Wasdale Head. We had another pint in the hotel, then back to the pub where Margaret had prepared a Sunday roast. A couple more pints at the bar, with the customers, and then to bed after a big, big day out. There would be so many big days ahead over the next few years.

At this time, I was having a big struggle with alcohol. I would decide to go dry for a week, but when the week was over I would binge as if to make up for the previous dry days. Some days I would go out climbing with the students, who studied at Charlotte Mason College, just up the lane from the pub. I often led a climb, but was so pissed I could not remember what climb it had been the next day.

Ian Wall asked me one day if I could help a friend of his guide some clients on the famous Cuillin Ridge on the Isle of Skye. I said I would, and two of the clients, a sweet couple, would pick me up early the next morning on their way north. Tony and I had been climbing that day. It was my birthday, so we started drinking. I was put to bed by about 10 o'clock, I was bladdered. The couple came to pick me up around 6 the next morning. I was still pissed, I don't know what they thought as I fumbled my way into the back of their van, remembering that I had wet the bed. Wracked with guilt, I fell into a deep sleep in the back of that van. As we came to Fort William, I woke up. The nice couple went shopping whilst I, feeling dreadful, sought out the nearest pub. After three pints of strong lager I felt like my old self again as we set off for Skye. God knows what they were thinking, but they never let on. I think they were too nice.

We stayed in the old school house in Carbost. There were seven clients, I think, and us two instructors. They were lovely people, so I was determined not to make a tit of myself.

We took them to the Chioch Stone, but the weather was appalling, so we backed off and decided to climb Blaven and Clach Glass at the south end of the Island. The sun had now come out, the scenery stunning. The party needed assistance from time to time, so I was happy to be there for them as we topped out both peaks. The trip had gone well, but I thought I had gotten away with murder.

There are times when a landlord must stamp his authority on a pub. As a newcomer I would be tested by a section of the local community. The local drunks, some of the local footballers, ("we're locals, and we can behave as we want"). Not in my pub boys. I was quite strict and got a reputation for being so. I was often called a miserable old bastard when ordering the unruly out. I even managed to tame visiting rugby clubs after a while. All I asked for was respect the house, they didn't have to like me.

One Friday before the Christmas break, (Black Eye Friday), I had been expecting trouble, but by 7 o'clock all was well. I left the bar and went upstairs for a bite to eat, but it was not long before I heard loud singing from below. About 12 locals had turned up, in their cups, and determined to cause trouble. Unfortunately, the staff had served them and they thought themselves established. Not so, I offered to refund them for their drinks on condition that they left immediately. They were not in agreement. I proceeded to relieve the first chap of his pint. He held on to his glass so tightly that he was on the floor before the glass was mine. Well, the rest of them took umbrage at this and set about me. All hell broke loose, fists were flying, eyes were being blackened, nosed bloodied as some of my customers piled in to help me. Someone said that the police had been called, so before they were able to throw me down the cellar steps they decided to leave. Margaret followed them into the yard, where they said "We love you Margaret, but we hate that bastard you're married to."

I went upstairs to change my shirt, which had been ripped from my back in the melee. Composed again and back behind the bar pulling a pint, when one of the buggers, a big lad returned. I thought he had come to apologise but no, he came behind the bar, and punched me right in the gob. I saw red, and all I could see was his big daft face grinning at me. I launched myself at him, and my forehead struck his nose full tilt. He fell to the floor bleeding and moaning. I had him in a half Nelson pushing hard up his back. He said, "Please, I'm dying." I said, "Yes, die you bastard." My customers were clapping, the police took him away and life returned to normal.

This was my first Christmas at the Rule. Margaret had decorated the place beautifully and it looked a treat.

I was drinking heavily but had a huge tolerance so could appear quite normal. I thought I had been born five pints under par.

We opened up for a couple of hours on Christmas Day, when I would stand drinks for my regulars, they were great and never abused our hospitality. On Christmas night we would open too for a couple of hours when we would play games and maybe do a quiz, all very nice.

Boxing day was a different matter. It was the traditional hunt, and whilst most people behaved well, a few saw it as an occasion to get shit-faced and belligerent. I hated it and was thankful when we shut the bar at 3 o'clock. I declined to open that evening to spare me the aggravation of having to deal with those arseholes. It's a shame, isn't it, when the few spoil it for the many. C'est la vie.

The pub was doing very well, but I was still drinking heavily and neglecting it, preferring to go visiting my landlord friends in Ulverston. We had just acquired a new car, a Ford Fiesta 1600 Ghia. I went visiting Mother's first, a whiskey and a couple of Valium to start with, then a gallop around the pubs in town to say hi to those good old boys. It was then time to return to Ambleside to open the pub before 5 o'clock. I never made it. On my way back, I decided to call in at Townhead to see my pal Charles Townley. Charles was always generous so we quaffed a very large Scotch together. I remember getting into the car, but nothing more.

The next thing I knew, as I became conscious, was that people were trying to extract me from the wreckage of what had been my car.

The car was only two months old, but was now just a ball of scrap. How I survived I will never know. However, I was put in an ambulance and was dropped off in Windermere Po-

1 Sharni, a hound with Zen quality
2 Margaret and me hosting our first new year party at the pub
3 Becs on my shoulder with Loughrigg behind
4 Becs as a toddler

5   Standing by to the compressor whilst at work. Photo: Paul Renouf
6   Me and the team building a council jetty at Waterhead, Windermere. Photo: Paul Renouf
7   Myself and Stephen Brew driving piles. Photo: Paul Renouf
8   Tony Greenbank, the journalist & gentleman
9   Me at work at Waterhead. Photo: Paul Renouf

lice Station. They were going to breathalyse me, but noticed blood coming from the corner of my mouth. An ambulance was summoned and I was whisked off to Kendal Infirmary where I was put to bed. The cause of the bleeding was that I had bitten the inside of my cheek in the crash (lucky me).

I was in my bed feeling very sorry for myself, I was battered and could barely move, and I could see that people were looking at me with disdain. Then all of a sudden, a moment of epiphany! A voice — from where I do not know — said to me, "Lockley, if this is what drink is doing to you, it's time you stopped." At that moment I stopped drinking. I started to go to AA meetings where they were so helpful, the knew the score, and taught me how to get straight in my head.

A whole new way of life was opening up for me, I could not believe how much time I had wasted in drinking and getting drunk. Had this not happened to me, I would have surely died many years ago.

The pub had been running well during my period of inebriation. Phil ran the bar during the day, and the dear students would be there for the evening shift, although I would be around like a stern father, malefactors would be summoned into the back room to be given a Lockley lecture. It was a right of passage for some of the younger ones, but it kept the old boat on an even keel.

I was now free of alcohol and the various diazepams. I felt renewed, life opened up before me. Mike Tullis, who had done work for me in my previous life, asked me if I would like to work for him as a sub contractor. I got my CSI certification and my pay was fourteen pounds a day. Not a lot, but I paid my barman ten pounds for his shift, so I reckoned I was in profit.

Now Mike Tullis is an engineer, and a highly skilled one too. We undertook all kinds of work from earth and rock moving, blasting, dredging and jetty building. We built boat houses, slipways and there are very few properties around Windermere and Coniston Water where we have not worked.

On Ullswater we rebuilt the steamer piers twice over the years, and we also laid a fibre optic cable along the bed of the lake for Telecom Marine. The cable weighed 17 tons and although these jobs were highly technical we could generally find a way to be competitive and we were always busy.

In one year we built over two miles of jetties and for the millennium we built a jetty which was a replica of a pier which had been at Seascale, in Victorian times. It ran out to sea, was one hundred yards long, built with Green Heart & Iroco, (resilient hard woods), and stainless steel. That pier is as good today as it was in 1999 when we built it.

I worked with Mike for about 20 years until he sold the business in 2000 to a guy called Richard Marsh. I worked for Richard for about 12 months, after which time I up sticks and went to Billy Slater at Jetties and Moorings Ltd. Billy and Barry and their gang were such fun to work with, and when young Nick Fieldhouse joined us I was delighted.

Nick and I worked with Mike Tullis previously. Mike would leave us to our own devices,

1. Woodford, Tim Hartley, and me on Scafell summit on a wet day
2. Me climbing over Hanging Bastion, Castle Rock, Thirlmere
3. Me climbing on White Ghyll, Langdale. Photo: Bill Birkett
4. Me climbing on White Ghyll, Langdale. Photo: Bill Birkett

1   John Hargreaves on Oxford and Cambridge route above Buttermere, the photo was taken by Bill Birkett. John, an accomplished climber and alpinist came to live in Ambleside from Blackpool.

2   Bill Peascod on the Great flake, Scafell. He was born in Maryport in 1920, he trained as a mining engineer and became a famous climber and landscape artist having moved to Australia in 1952. He returned to the Lakes in 1980 and continued climbing until his death whilst on Scafell in 1985, just a couple of weeks after becoming an OAP (Picture by Bill)

Nick was young, but very capable and we worked very well together. "We can do this Lockley," Nick would say, as 'No' was not a word in his vocabulary. He would take on seemingly impossible jobs that others dare not tackle.

At the time I started to work for Mike Tullis, I had also started climbing on a regular basis with my dear friend Tony Greenbank. Every weekend, we would go out in all weathers, and worked our way through all the classic climbs in the Lake District. These were exciting times, as the area was experiencing a renaissance in hard rock climbing. New routes were being put up, even Tony and I notched up one or two.

The Golden Rule became the hub of interest. The Fell and Rock Club would hold their guide book committee meetings here. The giants of the climbing and mountaineering world would call in for a few pints and a chin-wag around the fire. I need not mention names, all were here at this time.

3   Paul Cornforth an Ambleside lad climbing solo on "Tumbleweed Connection" in Borrowdale, he now builds climbing walls around the country.

4   Tony climbing on — I think — Kipling Grooves on Gimmer Crag. Photographer unknown.

I must, at this point, mention Tim Hartley and his son George. Tim was a teacher at a public school in Kent. He and the boy would come to the lakes during school holidays, and go climbing with Tony and me. They were such fun, after a day on the rocks we would retire to the Rule, drink beer, swap stories, then off to bed, full of beer and very happy.

Poor Tim died of a heart attack when he was only 50 years old. I miss him. George is now the headmaster of a big school in Chester.

One day Tony and I would go to a new climbing crag on Harter Fell above Hard Knott Pass where Al Phisackerley was looking for some new routes to climb.

I was driving my little Citroën 2 CV and as we were going along Wrynose Bottom, we were being held up by a nervous BMW driver who was several cars in front of us. We negotiated our way past these cars with some difficulty, and as we pulled alongside the "Beamer"

Tony pulled a face at the driver, then put his thumb to this nose and wiggled his fingers at him as we squeezed past.

At the head of the pass, there is a little pull-in which we reversed into. We were busy taking our climbing gear from the back of the little car, when the BMW came over the brow of the hill. It stopped and out of that car emerged a giant of a man who advanced toward Tony, who was now backing up the hill with a strange grin on his face. The big man was pointing at Tony, who was still in reverse and said, "You sir, are an ignorant fucking cunt." Seeing trouble ahead, I placed myself in between them and said to the big chap, in a voice as deep as I could muster, "Now settle down pal, no harm done," to which he responded, "Yes, you take a swing, I would just love that." I then held out my hand and apologised for upsetting him. He was appeased, the colour returned to Tony's face, the big chap got back in his car and we went our separate ways, thank God.

We arrived at the crag to see Al scampering around the crag in a pair of wellington boots. He was such a good climber. I went with him one day to Tarn Crags, above Easedale, which is behind the Lion and the Lamb, above Easedale Tarn, Grasmere. Whilst viewing the crag, we sat down for a sandwich and drink from out thermos. With us was my dog, Sharni, who had a Zen like quality and was a wonderful companion. She was sitting in a contemplative sort of way, with her nose regally sniffing the air and stunning scenery, when I offered her a sandwich. She examined my bland offering, and then slowly returned her gaze to the distant fells and politely rejected my kind offer. I said, "Eat that fucking sandwich." She complied immediately. Al was so impressed that the first route we climbed, we called "Sharni Slabs." This is still in the Fell and Rock guide books today. She was a Lurcher and enjoyed nothing more than coming out adventuring with the boys — she was one of the pack. If she was told to wait at the bottom of a climb, she would wait and not move. If she was invited to meet us at the top, she would find her way there and meet us with a wagging tail and big licks. This was an intelligent dog.

As Sharni got old she became ill and passed away in the pub, while I was at work. On my return, Al Risdon greeted me very sombrely, like an undertaker. He lead me to the back parlour, where poor Sharni lay, covered in a sheet. He gently lifted the sheet, so as to let me view the body. I found this almost funny. Bless them both.

CHAPTER 9

Hangover

Dove Crag is one of the most impressive pieces of rock in the Lake District. It dominates the head of Dovedale, a short valley which leads from the Fairfield massif, down to Brothers Water. On this auspicious day, Tony and I would venture out with a mind to climb Hangover, a 70m route which worked its way up the centre of the crag. A daunting proposition, hard and over hanging. But we are up for it. Our first mistake was to park in the Brothers Water campsite. After two minutes whilst putting on our rucksacks a pick up truck pulled up alongside, we had not asked permission and were told to leave the site in no uncertain terms. Fortunately we were able to park at Hartsop Hall, at the foot of the valley, the folks there were more amenable. An hours walk lead us to the base of the climb. We had to crane our necks to view the way. It was going to test us this route. Tony liked to lead the more difficult ones and I was happy to follow.

The first pitch of about 18 metres was fairly easy and lead to a large grassy ledge. With me securely belayed, Tony lead off up a steep corner, a 5a move. In this corner was a large crack in which Tony placed lots of protection. At the top of the corner one moved to the left onto a steep wall. Tony was now out of view, as he moved carefully up to the next stance.

"Climb when you are ready," came the call. So up the corner I started, removing Tony's runners as I went. At the head of the corner, I jammed my fist into the crack so as to have a good look at the wall around the corner. I could now see Tony some distance above me. I was impressed, this was hard and exposed climbing. Looking downwards I saw a man walking on a path which ran below us. Just as I was about to release my fist from the crack, the piece of rock I was on parted company with the crag. Swinging through the air, on a giant pendulum, trying to divest myself from my rocky companion, I was glad when it fell away from me. It made a crater as it stuck the ground, just in front of the man on the path. He looked up and shouted, "That's going to make it harder." As I swung back on the wall below Tony, I looked up at him and asked, "Have I gone white?" "White?" he said, "You have gone transparent!" The rope had held and we were safe, so on we went, much relieved.

The difficulties we encountered on that climb were relentless, so it was with great relief and pleasure that we shook hands on its completion. This was real adventure, it is in situations like this when one feels alive.

We had some good winter conditions in the 80's so ice climbing was the thing to do. Armed with axe, hammer and crampons, off we would set out down to conquer the classics. Some were very hard and technical, but Tony and I generally bossed them.

Absolutely brilliant I thought, although once I fell off a vertical ice pillar above Kirkstone Pass. I broke my wrist and nose and felt such a twat, as I made my bloody way down to the car park. "You OK," folk would say. "Never felt better," I would reply. I had been lucky, crampons & ice-axes can be a big hazard in a fall.

During this time dear Margaret was doing the books, and as I was working on the lake, paid little attention to the pubs finances, I was just the front man. I'm afraid Margaret got in a bit of a pickle, not wishing to reveal the situation, she buried her head in the sand as we sank deeper and deeper into debt. I found out when one morning Margaret told me the bank manager wanted a word. I went into his office and asked if there was some kind of problem. "A big one," he said, "At close of business yesterday you were £54,000 overdrawn." Well, I was a bit shocked, as you might imagine, and to make matters worse, there was a backlog of bills to be paid. Our total debts amounted to over £80,000, we were paying the bank £300 per week in interest alone. Even the bailiffs turned up one day. They didn't take anything, but made a list of our assets. This was very embarrassing.

At this time, a new customer turned up at the pub. Newly divorced and retired, Alan Risdon had worked in banking. He loved beer and was a stalwart CAMRA member. He wore clogs and was known as "Alan no socks."

This dear man offered to take over the book keeping and financial control. He placed £20,000 into the pub's account unilaterally, telling me to pay him back whenever I was able. Alan, a Quaker, was such a kind man who saved the day for the pub.

This episode taught me a lot. It is only money, I could have worried myself sick, but what would have been the point of that — nobody else gave a toss, so why should I.

I had been climbing with Tony one day, and on my return to the pub, walked into the bar where Margaret was talking to a family. With them was a pretty girl. "This is Vicky," said Margaret, "and she's going to work for us." Vicky had come to college here to do her degree and then to become a teacher. Well, Vicks and I got on like a house on fire, she had had a tough upbringing, and I think she saw in me a father she would have wanted. I started to take Vics climbing, she was a natural, so off to the climbing wall in Keswick we would go in the evenings. Driving back to Ambleside, we would talk, listen to music and started to become very close. Quite honestly, we fell for each other, but because of a 30 year age gap we never crossed the Rubicon. We had all sorts of adventures, nearly getting drowned in a Canadian canoe on the river Derwent, crashing into Grizedale forest when a hot air balloon we were in fell to earth, as we were trying to land it, and me hanging on to her legs when she took off in a paraglider, as I was worried she was about to fly away, and crash into the woods.

Vicky had an incredible enthusiasm for life, and was blessed with a mind that was as big as the universe. She would come back into my life many years in the future.

One evening on TV I saw a film about a French guy who climbed 3 of the big north faces in 24 hours. On the top of the Grande Jorass he opened a sack, pulled out a paraglider and flew off to the base of the next climb.

I was going to have to have a go at this, and as it happened, a friend of mine, dear John Barlowe, had arranged with a guy, Alan Scrace, to come to the lakes and teach us how to fly these paragliders. I was hooked from the start, got qualified and purchased my first glider. I think it cost me £350. More like a flying brick than a glider. It had a glide angle of about 4 to 1. (For every one metre I go down I go forwards four. Hopefully).

One day I took my glider to Bewaldeth, a nice grassy ridge near Bassenthwaite lake where the hang gliders often flew. As I drew near, I saw a pink, white and red paraglider soaring above the ridge. Oooh, I thought, this looks good, as I had only flown top to bottoms before.

I got about halfway up the side of the ridge where I thought there would be enough breeze to get me airborne. After a few failed attempts I finally got airborne. Well, fuck me, I was soaring like a bird. Up and down, along the ridge, riding the wind, and looking down on the earth for the first time on my glider.

The other glider had now landed on the ridge top, so clever me thought I would do the same. I had underestimated the speed of the wind on the ridge top, so as I landed, I was going backwards. Then my glider turned into a spinnaker, and started to propel me over the ground at great speed. I finally got the thing under control when the young man with the pink glider came over and introduced himself. Jocky Sanderson was 21 years old, 25 years my junior. "We will have to make some improvements on your ground handling," he said, and in this way, a long and close friendship was born.

Jocky's parents had a hotel in Stonethwaite, Borrowdale and he had come down from John Ridgeway's Adventure School, where he worked, to help them run the place. He had also started an outdoor adventure school, of his own, called Eagle Quest and would take clients out in all the sports that the Lake District could offer. Jocky was good, be it rock climbing, canoeing, sailing, or management development training. He could do the lot. And it was not long before I got roped in to help out. Jocky's heart was in the sky, and as paragliding was becoming more popular, Eagle Quest developed into a paragliding school. I was now a Trainee Instructor (official).

The training programme was quite structured and formal. One needed to be a member of the B.H.P.A. and satisfy them that one was competent. Then, there were four stages of qualification: Student Pilot, Club Pilot, Pilot, then Advanced Pilot. In order to teach, one had to be of Pilot rating as a minimum. One had to do written exams, go to residential courses in which we had to demonstrate our communication skills, and equally important demonstrate our ability in the air, which included cross country flying, knowledge of meteorology and be qualified in first aid. Quite a lot before we were let loose on the students.

1   Me flying at Pendle Hill for the benefit for the Yorkshire Evening Post
2   Jocky and I during the early days of working together, 1990
3   Jocks and I climbing Clough Head for a fly

4   Jocky, Jules and Barty launching a paraglider attached to a windsurf board during a windy January day

5   Me in my standard flying attire note the simple harness

By now Jocky was often in Europe, sometimes for competition, and sometimes to test gliders for the manufacturers. These tests were compulsory, and the gliders were graded as to the way they behaved. Safe student gliders attaining level 1 and performance competition gliders being level 3. So some gliders were tame, safe and easy to fly, and some were killers, fast but vicious!!

I have known some pilots who, not being particularly good themselves, got hold of performance machines. Then it wasn't the pilot flying the glider, but the glider flying the pilot. This could end up in tears, when the poor bugger would loose control and end up crashing and often in hospital. I once got a cheap glider from the Czech Republic, they weren't subjected to the standard European tests, so I took it on face value. It seemed great, but one day having fallen out with a girlfriend and being hung over, I took this glider to Bewaldeth. It was windy and gusting, so none of the pilots were flying, and were grounded, waiting for things to improve. Lockley knew better!

I launched the glider and shot skyward. I was making no forward progress, so I loosened off the trimmers. This gave me more speed, but made the glider less stable. The wing tips were now collapsing, but I still felt in control. I was now showing off (I had an audience). I pushed on the speed bar to give me more speed, increasing the glider's instability. The wing was now collapsing in a threatening way. I still felt in control and wondered how could I make it go even faster. This was the straw that broke the camels back. I had pushed hard on the front risers when all hell let loose. 80% of the glider folded up, dropped violently to my right, and started to go into a nose-down spiral, which I tried to control by braking what little remained of the left wing that was still flying, causing that bit of wing to stall and then spin. I had clearly over-corrected and things were not looking good. I let the brake off which allowed the wing to dive again, violently nose diving, to regain balanced flight. The ground was rushing towards me. I thought this was going to hurt, then nothing, utter nothing.

I came to, strange noises were going on in my head and a circle of people were looking down at me. "Have I crashed?" I asked. "Yes," they said, as they assessed me and my injuries. I kept asking the same question, "Did I crash?" This was a sign I was concussed. They took me to Keswick hospital where the doctors gave me a clean bill of health.

However, when I got back home I knew things were not right, so I got into my car, with much pain and difficulty I might say. I presented myself at Kendal A&E. X-Rays showed that I had broken three bones in my hand, three broken ribs, and four vertebrae had been displaced in my neck. They put me in a collar dead quick. I had been extremely lucky. I could have died that day. I have to say that the fault was not with the glider, but with the pilot, who should have known better!

When the weather was bad, when we couldn't fly or climb, we would turn to fun on the water. We would go Beck Bottoming, which is a form of Ghyll scrambling, but when the becks were in spate. This was exciting, if not a bit dangerous sometimes. Our wetsuits

1   Me with my dislocated shoulder in a sling post a canoe trip with Collin Downer and Jocks on the Upper Derwent, (disaster)
2   Me teaching at Silecoft we needed strong winds with such bad glider to soar
2   Jocks and me teaching
3   Jocks and I formation flying on our state-of-the-art Falhawk Athletes, aka Fold Hawks

would keep us snug, so we could spend hours braving the torrents, egging each other on and generally goofing around.

I mentioned earlier about a canoe trip on the river Greta, that runs through Keswick. We put in at Threlkeld, Vicks and I in a Canadian, and the rest of the boys in kayaks. The water was very high and wild so on several occasions we had to get to shore to empty the boat. Whilst negotiating a particularly strong rapid our canoe filled and sank beneath us. Pat McVey came alongside us and towed Vicks to safety. I tried to stay with the craft, but she disappeared beneath me, and I found myself being thrashed in the torrent.

I was exhausted but managed to escape on a bend under a steep bank. I found it nearly impossible to climb up it. I then saw there were stables at the top of this bank. I had been climbing a midden, a pile of horse pooh, that came from Calvert trust horse stables. However, I did make it back to the gang, who had been waiting in a worried kind of way and who were pleased to see me. The feeling was mutual.

Jocky was spending more time in France, be it competing or testing. Paragliding was getting more popular, so Eagle Quest became very busy. I spent most weekends running the school with my dear friend Barty (Ian Bartrum). It was so rewarding to see how quickly people would progress, Barty and I ran a pilot production line, and although it was a huge responsibility we would deal with a dozen students at a time.

Eagle Quest was expanding, we bought a winch from a school in London, this was to enable us to tow gliders into the air on days when there was little wind. Jocky and I would do a test flight, Jocks on the glider, me on the winch. Well, I wasn't too sure how this thing was controlled so I gave it full bat. Jocks was out of sight when I started to wind the line in.

Jocks appeared over the skyline, shooting heavenward like a rocket. I was on full revs, with the drum winding in furiously, and the glider was nearly above me. I heard my friend say "Fucking hell" on the radio as he came overhead. As the glider started to lift the winch with me on it, I let go of the throttle. This allowed Jocks to release the line and resume normal flight. God, when I think back, I could have been facing an air accident tribunal, but for our inevitable luck, and the grace of the aforementioned.

Another wet and sorry weekend, so we decided to navigate the river Greta in the Borrowdale Valley. We put in at Seathwaite, Jocky, Colin Downer, me and Julian, Jocky's brother. As I went over a small weir I capsized and found myself upside down. Unfortunately, my elbow struck a rock, which caused my shoulder to dislocate. I rolled upright and called to Colin, "I've dislocated my shoulder." "Don't talk fucking silly," said Colin, "get yourself over here." "I have, honest," said I, as I up righted myself again. Realising my plight, Colin came to my rescue. A painful walk across the field led to the road, and a bridge where the river flowed through.

Colin had just done a big first aid course, so he had me lay on the bridge, with arm hanging down. After a brief examination, he declared, "Nope, John, definitely not dislocated." I said, "Colin, it definitely fucking is."

By now Jocky had arrived in the Land Rover when I was taken to Keswick Hospital, where a young lady doctor was on duty. "I'll pop it back in for you" she said. Not so, she pulled, twisted, and pushed as I grunted and hollered, and after about 20 minutes she admitted defeat and sent me to Carlisle Infirmary with Jocks where a team would be waiting for us. Fortunately the nice doctor had given me a shot of pethidine, so our journey to Carlisle hadn't been too painful.

As promised, a team was waiting for us, three men and a blanket. They decided that a good dose of Valium would help matters, so after a few minutes, I was feeling grand. These guys placed the blanket round me, two of them holding the ends, on my opposite side the other guy got hold of my arm. Well, they pulled and twisted, pulled and twisted and all to no avail. They apologised and told me I would have to go to the operating theatre where, yet another team, would be waiting. They were ready for me, told me to lay on the floor where they put me to sleep. I woke up in bed feeling as if both shoulders had been dislocated. I looked at my injuries and noted a large boot shaped bruise under my armpit, I asked the consultant what this was. "Well John, in order to reduce your shoulder we had to be quite brutal. While you were on the floor, my colleagues provided resistance to the traction, by securing your other side, while I was pulling your arm, with both hands, and my feet in your armpit and neck, while another colleague sat on your chest for anchorage." Basic, brutal, but effective.

During my convalescence I regularly went flying with Jock's dad who had the use of a little Cessna 104, which he kept at Carlisle airport. He was often short of cash, so if I filled her up with fuel, he would let me fly her. What fun we had, we went all over the lakes, over to Barrow, and around Morecambe Bay. John Sanderson was a good pilot, and I am grateful to him for those airborne experiences. I don't think he paid hangar fees. He told me that if one had the use of an aircraft, one must be wealthy.

Every summer we would take the students to France where they could learn to fly in the mountainous Alps, in much stronger and testing environments. My first alpine flight was at Saint Hilaire, a small take-off field ended with a 1500' sheer drop to the landing field below.

I was so keen to get airborne, I struck a tree stump with my harness and broke the plywood seat, it certainly gave me something to think about during my half hour flight.

Alpine flying is so exciting, the air can be sometimes as smooth as silk, generally in the mornings and evenings, but when it becomes thermic and unstable it can be rough as hell.

Screaming towards cloud base at 10,000 feet in a strong thermal certainly concentrates the mind, especially if you feel its pull too strong. Flying out of a big thermal can be tricky as the glider passes from warm rising air into the cold sinking air around it. A collapse of some kind can be almost guaranteed. Most accidents happen when in this situation. The pilot over compensates with his controls and changes the kind friendly wing into a raging beast which will not be tamed. At this point, he might throw his reserved chute and leave the rest of his flight in the lap of the gods.

Jocky and Hamish had been out to a competition in France. Hamish was the skipper of a trawler called '*Defiance.*' He fished for langoustine and prawns in the waters around the Isle of Skye. Whilst he had been away, his crew had been busy with heavy catches and wanted some time off, so Jocky volunteers himself and me to go fishing for a week.

They were on their way north when they phoned me, which gave me only a few hours to pack and make arrangements to cover during my absence.

They picked me up around 7pm and we headed north arriving at Kyle in the early morning. After a quick breakfast we dashed around the supermarket for our stores. Jocky said we wouldn't need too much as we would be eating fresh fish. Hamish told him to put that idea straight out of his head. With enough food to last us for a week, we headed off for Carbost on the Isle of Skye where *Defiance* was berthed.

This was a working trawler, about 80ft long and built to catch fish. On board was Kenny, Hamish's 1st mate, it would be Kenny who would show us the ropes.

The stores were lowered from the jetty, then we followed down the ladder and onto the deck, the new crew. May the lord be with us!!

The first thing I noticed was the smell. Strong and pungent and present throughout the boat. Our quarters were at the stern, down a ladder and into a damp, smelly, steel cave. Across the transom were freezers, a cooler, sink and cupboards, our kitchen, a big table occupied the centre of this dark, damp place, which was to be our home for the next few days. Sleeping berths were fitted down each side of the room, when lying in them your nose was no more than 6 inches from the upper bunk, they were very claustrophobic and everything felt so damp. Having selected our chosen places, stowed our gear, went back up the ladder, ready to start work.

Hamish was already heading for the fishing grounds, so Kenny started to explain what our duties would be. Firstly, the net is shot at the stern, then the otter boards, (gates), have to be fixed to the towing cables on each side of the mouth of the net, (these keep the net open). The cables are then run out until the net is several hundred yards behind the boat, being towed along the sea bed, hopefully catching langoustine.

After about three hours the net is hauled back to the boat, the otter boards detached, then the net is manoeuvred to the side of the boat where the 'cod end' (where the fish are) is hoisted aboard and the catch released onto the deck.

The process is repeated when the net is shot once again. This gives us four hours to sort, wash and stow the catch, eat and rest, before the next haul is released, and the process started again.

Our first haul was very poor and we had cleared it in just over an hour. Jocky thought this was going to be easy, but Hamish had decided to look for better fishing grounds in the Minch. As we were making our way there, we were able to grab some food and a cuppa, and to learn a little more of what was expected of us.

Make no mistake, this is a hard and dangerous job, so we had to learn fast because lives depended on us, no shit. Having said this, there was no toilet on board, so we had to do our

1   *Defiance* the trawler on a sea festival day on Skye
2   *Defiance*
3   Jocky and I sailing *Defiance* across to Ireland to fly

jobbies in a bucket, making sure that it was first wetted so that the turds didn't stick. One would try to sneak away and squat behind the winches, but there would always be someone who would gleefully take a snapshot of whoever might be crapping.

The first haul would be shot around 3 in the morning, this would give us time to get breakfast, wash and prepare ourselves for the day ahead. By 6 o'clock the first net-full would be aboard and the net shot once again.

This was now the routine, shoot the net, haul it in, empty it onto the deck, shoot it again, sort the catch, haul the net etc. etc.

The catches were now quite big and the boat would keel over as the cod end was hauled aboard. We had little time between sorting the catch before the next haul would be winched aboard. We learned very quickly how to make the most of the few free minutes between catches we would get. We brewed tea and made sandwiches at break-neck speed. I think the latest we were working was one o'clock in the morning. Sleep came very easily, we were lucky to get four hours each night. Hamish, whilst searching for good fishing grounds would only get two hours. How he did it I don't know, a very hard man.

On the third day we had to go to Portree to unload our catch, we had been so busy. We pulled alongside a little fishing boat owned by 'fire eater' Dave Rawlings, one of the sweetest men I have known, wonderfully human, hilarious when drunk and kind when sober. We joined him below where we shared a few beers and stories of past days, (he was with us when we went to the Czech Republic to see those gliders).

All too soon, we left the fire eater and his son Neil, and steamed away to the fishing grounds.

Whilst at sea, we would share the cooking. I do not normally cook, but on this occasion I conjured up a beef stew followed by a creamy rice pudding with a sweet brown crust on top. We had to fit this in with our other duties, and as the meal was well received I felt very pleased with myself.

One afternoon, we were hauling in the net when all of a sudden we started to go backwards. Jocky and I were at the stern and became quite alarmed as the sea was about to come over the deck. Quick as a flash, Hamish stopped the boat, Kenny stopped the winches and we were safe. Another trawler, some distance behind us had gone over our nets and it was quite a while, with much cussing and swearing over the radio, before we were free. Fortunately there was no damage done, a tonne of fish came aboard, and back to work we went.

By the end of the fifth day we had caught enough and headed back to the Kyle where we would unload our catch and Hamish would get paid. The boat gets half, then Hamish got half the balance, and half of that was Kenny's, with Jocky and I getting the rest. Twas a great deal of money in those days as we received £500 each.

That night we went out to the pub and were invited to the Saturday Ceilidh in the village hall. Eee, it were grand fun, and on Sunday morning we woke up with rather sore heads.

Jocky and I were ready to go south but on the Sabbath public transport is almost non-existent on the west coast. Hamish saved the day by flagging down a guy in a red Vauxhall Cavalier as he came over the Skye bridge. This wee fellow was going to Edinburgh, which suited us fine. Now this poor chap, to say the best, was not a good driver. I don't think he had been away from the island very often, so after a frustrating half hour, I asked him if he would like me to drive for a while. He was delighted at this idea. Well, I like driving fast and I like overtaking. This Cavalier was about to be put through its paces. As we sped along, the wee fellow became very quiet, he looked like he was having a bad indigestion but was too polite to ask me to slow down. We got to Edinburgh in no time, thanked the trembling islander and boarded the train south.

We had now become established as a paragliding school and started to travel. We went to Thailand as guests of their hang gliding club, to Turkey on a regular basis and often to the Alps.

Oludeniz in Turkey is a fine holiday resort. A huge mountain Babadag rears up from the sea, so if you take off from the summit you have 6000ft of air underneath you by the time you are over the sea. This is an ideal place for advanced training and the whole resort is geared up for paragliding.

Thailand was wonderful, Mr Narint hosted us, we visited many places and saw many things. Bangkok was both horrid and wonderful. My worst experience was when, under peer pressure, I took a girl to my hotel room. This was no girl but an old hag, "Why you no want me," she protested as I ushered her out of the door. It still cost me 1500 baht to be rid of her.

Over the years, so many young and beautiful young ladies came to work behind the bar whilst at college. Two girls, Kat and Karen stand out in my memory, the customers loved them because they put so much effort into entertaining them. I missed them terribly when they left to become successful teachers. I wish them well wherever they are now.

Jocky and I had enjoyed our time at sea and we started to think it would be great if we had a boat of our own. This boat would be called *Defiance*. A friend or ours, Dave Leaver, also a paraglider, ran a tourist boat out of Oban. He told us of a boatyard at a little place called Balvicar on the Isle of Seal. Jocky, Andy Ditchfield and me were to have a share each in our boat, if we found one and find one we did. *Defiance*, as she was now to be called, was sitting in a cradle on a hard standing. She looked to be a strong craft and a good sea boat. She was a Galleon 28, built in 1974. A sloop, with a hefty fin keel, beamy, and very strong. She was made in fibreglass, had a 20-horsepower Saab diesel engine, could sleep six people and had a roomy, well-protected cockpit. This would be the boat for us.

We paid £12,000 for her and would pick her up after the boatyard had anti-fouled her and made her ready for sea.

On that first week in April 1999, Jocky and I rolled into the boatyard. *Defiance* sat on her mooring in Balvicar Bay, she looked beautiful and inviting as we were rowed out to her. We spent our first night on her, she was roomy and comfortable, and we felt happy and snug, we stowed our stores away, studied what charts we had, enjoyed a couple of nightcaps, then settled down to sleep. It was still dark when we awoke to a beautiful starlit dawn, there was a red glow to the east, but we thought little of it. We made ourselves a good breakfast, got the weather forecast NE which didn't seem too bad, up to force 5, fine and with good visibility. We started the engine, slipped the mooring and headed out of the bay.

Port Patrick here we come! It was a lovely still frosty morning. The sun was shining and the sea as calm as glass. As we left the bay and came into the sound of Jura, a breeze picked up, so we set the sails. The engine was turned off, the sails were full and we felt top dollar as we headed south.

We passed by the dreaded Gulf of Corryvreckan, intrigued by the swirling waters and by now the wind was picking up a bit. We took in some sail, but were becoming a bit concerned. Clyde Coastguard were still forecasting force 5, may be 6. As we passed Craighouse, we thought it to be more like a 7. We pressed on, it was now late in the afternoon and blowing hard. The sea had a good chop on it and Jocky's dad phoned to say there was a gale warning out.

It was now getting dusk, the weather was worsening, and we didn't fancy going through the night in a gale, on a boat we were still getting to know. We saw from the charts there were some council moorings near the ferry ramp on the Isle of Gigha. We would pick up one of these. This was no easy task. The moorings were quite close in, there was an on-shore wind. We were now in a gale and on a rough sea. We had taken in the sails and were under engine power. We had to come in between the moorings and the rocky shore, then head into wind and hopefully pick one up. This we did at the first attempt, (full marks Jocks). While attaching the mooring I was leaning on the guard rail, which snapped! Jocky grabbed my legs as I was falling head first into the raging sea. We both held firm and I crawled up to the deck. We were safe, although the sea was now breaking over the boat. It was now dark, and the locals had driven onto the ferry ramp to get a peek at us poor buggers in the headlamps.

We had accidentally left our steaming light on at the mast head. The coastguard thought us to be a vessel in difficulty and radioed us at 1.00am, asking us if we were okay. We told them we were, they said the would then let us get back to sleep. We told them we weren't fucking sleeping.

As dawn broke the next day, things were improving a little, we had survived a wild night. Things had been thrown around the cabin, we had shared anchor watch, 2 hours on, 2 hours off and had learned a lot about the boat and about ourselves. We had come through.

Getting off the mooring wasn't easy, there was still a big swell, the tide had risen, so the mooring line only went slack when the bough dipped beneath the waves and that was the only time I could loose a turn on the fore cleat. After about 15 minutes we were free, my hands were frozen, but fortunately still intact. The weather improved, the sun was up, the wind eased, the waves calmed and we were in full sail again. *Defiance* picked up her skirts and we were off.

It's funny how one forgets the horrors of the previous night. We were happy now, and full of expectation on meeting Andy when we arrived at Port Patrick.

Port Patrick is a beautiful little harbour, hiding behind a rocky headland, where a narrow channel leads us in. Leading lights guide us, one of then high up in the village high street, which must be lined up with the other, lower one, on the harbour wall.

Andy was waiting for us, so we went to the Crown Hotel for a well earned dinner. For the previous 2 days there had been no thoughts of going for a poo, as I entered the Crown Hotel, things became a bit pressing, so I excused myself and went to attend to natures call. I think it must have been a smelly one as a voice from the urinal, in the broadest Scot's accent, bellowed, "It's fucken, munging in here. Is that you?" He said to a little chap having a pee. Not wishing him to be beaten, I felt I had to confess. "I'm sorry," I said from the cubical, "it was me, I haven't been for a couple of days, I've been at sea." "What the fuck have they been feeding yah?" he said. "Rats," I replied. He seemed to be satisfied with that response and the the door closed.

The Crown boasts a fine menu and we ate well whilst recounting our adventures of the past days we spent the night on *Defiance*, had a huge breakfast in the Harbour Café and did a few jobs on the boat as we waited for the evening tide. Jocks and Andy were heading for Whitehaven, where *Defiance* would be berthed, I was to drive Andy's car back and to meet them there. I watched them leave, jumped into the car when I realised I had left my glasses on board.

The road signs meant nothing to me, I was driving blind and on instinct. I managed to find the main road and met them in Whitehaven the next day. *Defiance* was at her new home and waiting for her next adventure.

Jocks and I decided we were going to take this sailing lark seriously, so we called upon John Crosby, who had been a Commander in the navy and who was now running the Calvert Trust, to school us in the art of seamanship. Our day skippers ticket, to be precise.

We were soon nipping across to the Isle of Man and during summer, took a cruise along the Clyde and west coast (in calmer waters than our last trip). We took a mooring and hired a cottage at Lochranza. Jocky's partner Kate and the boys sailed up with us and Margaret came up in the BMW so that we could tour the island. Arran is a lovely place, and we were lucky enough to enjoy good weather. This is apart from the midges, the little bastards.

Becky was by now at Lancaster University, and I don't think she ever set foot on *Defiance*. I was working on Lancaster Canal at this point. I had a British Waterways tug boat which propelled a barge on which was fixed an excavator arm. Becky was living in town, so it gave me the opportunity to spend time with her. She has always been a good daughter and I love her dearly.

In the early summer of 2000 we sailed *Defiance* to Ireland. We were heading for Strangford Loch, but as the tide was too strong at that time, we put in at Ardglass, a little fishing port, just south of the Loch. We were walking back from the pub when we noticed our boat drifting away. The local kids had let go our lines, the little buggers. As *Defiance* slipped into the night, the three of us quickly drew straws, and it was poor Andy who had to strip too his boxers and swim to grab a line and tow her back to his waiting crew-mates. Brrrr.

We entered the loch on a flowing tide. The current is very strong as it passes through the narrows, so we were going like a steam train. We found it very exciting as we thundered along. Strangford Loch is massive, with pretty villages dotted along its shores.

We took the bus to Belfast one day, it was quite an eye opener. I had been to the north some years earlier when I took a friend who was to run the Riverside Theatre at Coleraine. Although all the people we met were lovely, one could feel the tension in Belfast.

When we headed for home, there as some heavy weather approaching from the north. We sailed at night and went south round the Isle of Man to avoid the worst of the gale. As we were about to round the south of the island a killer whale came under the boat and stayed with us for a couple of minutes. This was magic. Jocky had been on watch most of the night, so I took over so that he could get some kip.

As we rounded the Calf of Man I headed NW but got hit by some heavy trailing seas, we were being slammed. When we hit the big waves, they were so violent that Jocky was thrown from his bunk. As he was trying to sleep, I decided to bear away to the west for a more comfortable ride. This worked, although we had to make up the lost ground later.

Fortunately, the weather improved so we swung round on a more northerly tack, the sun came out so we found ourselves on a broad reach with a sparkling sea. A school of porpoises joined us for a while, blowing merrily as they glided over the waves.

This was our longest trip to date, I think it was about 30 hours. *Defiance* had looked after us very well. As I'm writing I find that I miss her. She was a funny looking old girl, but she was sound.

During that summer Whitehaven hosted the tall ships and there's a festival, we had a ringside seat in the marina. Anna came up from London, the Crosby's came and friends called by. With fireworks, brass bands playing and tall ships around us, it was a fine display. I met Anna through paragliding, we became firm friends and have remained so for many years. I value her wisdom and her kind heart.

One day when out for a sail we had to anchor off the harbour as there wasn't quire enough water to get us into the lock, (spring tides). We were enjoying ourselves having a beer, and sun bathing when we spotted what looked like a large vessel coming over the horizon. Well, this ship got bigger and bigger as she came nearer, she was a cruise ship, and when she was a couple of hundred yards from us, to a loud clanking and rattling noise, her anchors were dropped. What would a cruise ship be doing here? After about a quarter of an hour, a large square hole appeared in the side of the ship and little orange craft started to spill out, it was as if she was having babies.

These little craft were full of passengers, and as there was enough water they were heading for the lock gates. We quickly pulled up our anchor, started the engine and went to join them in the lock. In the morning Whitehaven was waiting. The brass band was out again, the Morris dancers were banging sticks and the Mayor with his council stood to attention as the band played the Star Spangled Banner, after which the Mayor, in his official regalia, welcomed the guests then ushered them to their waiting coaches, when they were whisked away on a quick tour of the western Lake District, I guess.

The last long trip I made with Jock and *Defiance*, I remember very well. It was early in February. We were in Douglas bay, I was at the Tiller, under engine power and just heading her steady into the wind. We were waiting for a freighter to depart the docks. Jocks was on the radio to the harbour master who told us that it was gusting 60 knots at the pier head.

It was rough, spray was breaking over the bough and stinging my face. "What the fuck am I doing here," I thought. I was feeling miserable, we had a rough night passage from Whitehaven to the Isle of Man and it was Jocks' intention to sail to Ireland. Only three days previously I had been discharged from hospital after surgery for a hernia repair. I was in pain, both physically and mentally. I felt very sad, a beautiful affair I had been having for some time was breaking down, so not only were my stitches pulling, but my heart strings also. Good sex is wonderful, bad sex is totally demoralising, so perhaps one might understand how I was feeling.

The freighter passed us by as we made our way to the shelter of the quay. After making fast we walked into town to get a bite to eat. Poor Jocks could do nothing to lighten my mood, so with the best will in the world, I was not able to shake off my melancholia.

We retired to our bunks and downed a couple of beers as we were planning to head for Ireland on the morning tide.

Morning broke fresh with a still northerly breeze. We were close hauled and making slow progress and it was at this point that I told Jocks that I wanted to go home. I knew he was pissed off but was too gracious to show it, if we had run into heavy weather, I dare say that the surgeons good work might have been undone.

An uncomfortable if uneventful passage led us home and as I drove back to Ambleside I felt bad for Jocks as I had ruined his holiday. A good dear friend, this lad never reproached me or held this miserable episode in my life against me.

At this time a new manager came to run the Queens Hotel in town. I would call by for a half of beer and could see that this guy was top dollar, John Wrennall was a professional and I told him if he ever felt like changing jobs he must come to see me. It was about 12 months later when John reminded me of the conversation we had had.

He was ready to join us at the Rule and I was certainly ready to welcome him aboard, it did not take long for John to make big differences at the pub, and after 25 years, the pub was being run on a proper business like footing, (deep joy).

I cannot say how much I appreciate the difference John's efforts have made, and had he not been with us, I would have retired ten years ago.

Phillip and I were coming to our 75th birthdays, and as he loves train journeys, I arranged a tour of the alpine railways as a treat. Five weeks before the trip Phillip decided to have a massive heart attack. He was pulled from the car, "dead as a hammer." A trainee nurse, 18 years old, who lived nearby, was summoned. She worked on him for 15 minutes, and still no pulse. At this time a police car turned up with a defibrillator aboard. 20 minutes had now passed when they applied the device, and as if by a miracle, life returned, when he told them to "fuck off and leave me alone." A helicopter had now arrived, and he was flown to hospital in Truro. He owes his life to that little girl, though she did break eight of his ribs. Phillip was placed in a coma for two weeks, after which made a full and total recovery, although this had scuppered our little holiday. Not to worry about that, it's just so good to have him still with us.

CHAPTER 10

Ballooning Years

Over the years I have been lucky enough to enjoy a few hot air balloon adventures. In 1974 a friend of mine had a cousin who wanted to bring his balloon to the lakes. As I was using propane gas to run my forklifts, I was invited to go along, provided I supplied the gas to fuel the flights.

Getting airborne is a bit complex. Firstly, the balloon has to be unfolded, then rolled out over the ground. The basket and burner laid down sideways with the burner facing the balloon mouth. The suspension lines are attached, then a fan forces air into the flaccid envelope, making sure the crown at the top of the balloon is secure. The crown is a flap attached by Velcro, and connected to the basket by a line which can be pulled when hot air is needed to be released quickly. Crew members hold the mouth open when the pilot lights the burners. The hot air starts to inflate the balloon until she starts to slowly rise. Once fully inflated and ready to lift off the passengers then climb into the basket and the crew provide weight by holding on from the outside. When the pilot is ready, the crew are told to release. And the craft rises majestically heavenward. The crew then follow the flight from below.

The altitude of the craft is controlled by the use of the burners, so the hotter the balloon gets, the higher she will go. When the burners are turned off, flight is totally silent. One glides along at a chosen altitude when the sounds from the world below drift up to us.

On that first flight, we took off at Kendal and landed at Ulverston, having demolished a farmer's wall before coming to rest. The farmer was assured that we were properly insured.

It was not until the nineties when I flew again. Robbie lived in Windermere and had a balloon. 'Autumn Gold,' she was called, and Robbie, her owner, was a very adventurous pilot. So long as I worked for him on the ground, I would get corresponding time in the air. I remember one morning, having taken off in Wasdale, passing over Scafell about 10 feet above the summit whilst talking to the walkers as we floated by. They were gob smacked, and we felt very superior.

Whilst passing over fir plantations at tree top height, we would grab a tree top, hang on to it as long as we could, then let go. The old basket would get a good old swing going.

Robbie was training for his commercial licence, so this meant that he had to be under an instructor, co-piloting a much bigger balloon which could carry 12 passengers. We set off a bit late in the day from Swirls car park which is on the flanks of Helvellyn above the head of Thirlmere. As there was plenty of room in the basket, Vicks came along for the ride, always ready for an adventure that girl. I was ground crew, so I watched them head south along that lovely valley, I jumped into the 4 x 4 and followed their progress from below. The flew over Grasmere, over Loughrigg, then put down at Chapel Stile, in Langdale, where I joined them.

The balloon was sitting there swaying gently in the light breeze. I replaced some used gas bottles, one of the passengers swapped with me, I climbed into the basket and we were off. Vicks thought this great fun as we floated by Coniston Old Man at around 1500 feet. At this point, I noticed some dry grass and bits of wool gently rising by the side of the basket, sounds from below were becoming quite audible. I knew what was going on. Boys. I said, it's getting thermic, and the air was loosing its stability. This is not good as far as ballooning goes, (balloons like to fly in quiet, still air), and the boys were looking worried. We were approaching the Grizedale Valley now and were looking to land as quickly as possible. Most of the fields had ewes with lambs in them, but one was empty of stock. As we approached this field a thermal caught us and took us skyward. We dropped out of this one and were able to make another attempt. The balloon was now cooling and we were descending quite quickly.

The pilot and co pilot were arguing as to what action to take when another thermal caught us and, although the balloon was cold, we were going up. We were heading towards the forested hillside when we left the thermal and found ourselves in cold descending air and heading toward the fellside at about 10 mph. The boys were now burning full blast to try to stop our rapid fall. "We're going to crash," said Vicks, as the boys were now shouting at each other. "No, no," said I, "we won't crash." The basket hit the fellside hard, we were hanging on. The balloon, having lost the weight of the basket and passengers, because of the impact, leapt into the air with a giant bounce. It dramatically rose to more than 50 feet, before crashing to the ground again, as the boys hauled frantically on the crown line to release the now warmed air from the envelope. She bounced one more time before coming to rest. The basket was badly damaged but had protected us. We were on one side of a deer fence, and the now flaccid balloon was on the other.

We were shaken and bruised but okay. Vicks was the first to speak. "You're all fucking mad," she said. Probably true. It took a great deal of effort to extricate the debris from the fellside and onto the trailer.

On another occasion, we would take off at Low Wood, Windermere, in front of the hotel. It was a very quiet day, the lake was mirror still and there was no breeze. The balloon was inflated, we climbed aboard and with a little application of heat we were floating about a foot above ground. QNH is the term used when setting the altimeter (Query nautical height). The Low Wood sits at about 150 feet above sea level, so we would set the altimeter at zero but Robbie mistakenly (unlike him) set it at 150 feet, which is QFE (Query Field Elevation), the actual height above sea level). So when our altitude was 150 feet the altimeter read 300 feet. This would cause us some fun later. We were static, so we got some kind people to push us to the end of the jetty, (one I had built in earlier times). We then gave her some heat and we lifted skyward. At 1500' we were still in the same place over the lake so we went to 2000' to see if we could get some movement in the air. At 2500' we were going nowhere, only up. When Robbie decided to practice a cold descent. This technique allows the balloon to fall very quickly and requires a great deal of skill to control of the aircraft in the descent.

At the chosen moment, the pilot starts the burners full chat in order to slow the balloon enough to make a soft landing. Trouble was, we were 150' lower than we thought when the burn commenced (QFE, QNH). Oh bugger he cried, as the basket hit the lake. Water came pouring in through the sinking basket as we climbed up onto its rim. At this point, the balloon freed of its load and charged with a large dose of hot air, set off in the direction of up at great speed. At about 3000' she slowed and stopped her ascent. We found a little breeze from the north and put down with no more adventures at Newby Bridge. I am grateful for those wonderful times, and on looking back consider myself to be very lucky.

As the reader will know, Nick Fieldhouse and I had been working together for some years. Nick was always interested in fast cars and around the turn of the century, started importing "Lancia Intergrales" from Italy. He would posh them up to showroom condition and then sell them on. I would join him from time to time on a test drive. By God, he was a fast driver — how fast, I dare not say. His spatial awareness was incredible, so I never felt nervous as his passenger. He also imported "Mitsubishi Evos," and I would go with him to Carlisle to have them registered. On our return to Ambleside we were doing 145mph over Dunmail Raise, and I thought, "Ah well, so far, so good," as we sped past everybody.

Nick fancied doing a bit of off-road adventuring. There are many bridleways and green lanes in the lake district and some of them are very rugged and difficult to navigate by vehicle. Most would find them impassable. Our first adventure was a route over Garburn Pass, a bridleway that runs from Troutbeck to Kentmere. I was working in the bar when Nick appeared and asked if I fancied a run out. He had acquired a Jeep Wrangler which had a four litre engine under the bonnet.

We set off up the track and were soon to find ourselves facing a steep wall of rock. "We won't get over that," said I. "Just you watch me," said Nick. Oh so slowly he inched forward and upward, guiding the beast on. It was as if it had hands and feet, I could hardly believe what I was seeing. More obstacles confronted us and one by one they were overcome. The decent into Kentmere was just as hazardous, it would have been easy to overturn the jeep and have it fall down the slope beneath us. Nick was on it and even I was impressed. With more off-road adventures planned, Nick decided to buy a Land Rover racer from the Symonite Family, who had a garage near Bradford.

This vehicle was very basic. Four wheels with big tyres, a powerful engine and a strong chassis, two seats and a fuel tank. That being about it, apart from a roll cage for our protection! It was in February when we picked up the racer, we drove it back to Windermere in pouring rain, and as we were completely at the mercy of the elements, we were almost hypothermic when we arrived, another day to remember.

Our first adventure with the racer, was to navigate the track from Coniston to Seathwaite in the Duddon Valley. The trail starts easily enough, until one comes to the "rock gates," a narrow cleft which has to be negotiated with great care. The route rises and twists as it passes between these rock walls and the driver has to be inch perfect as he passes through. At this point many turn back, but the best is yet to come. The trail eases then, until one has to pass over a very narrow bridge which spans the beck that comes from Goats Water. After the bridge, the way steepens and climbs up to the col at Brown Pike. This is a tester for any driver as it becomes almost vertical for the last few yards as one tops out. With Dow Crags to our right, and the great sweep of Seathwaite before us, we descend into the Duddon Valley. The track contours some very steep slopes initially and then levels off, still descending and deeply rutted. A stone wall now runs parallel to the trail which turns right and leads to a fell gate through which we must pass. This gate is very, very narrow, and the way before us seems to be impassable. It is like glacial debris, just stones and boulders with deep bog on each side. A survey would have to be made on foot, and after some consideration, Nick decided it would go. Bearing in mind that if we had got stuck there it would have been almost impossible to rescue the vehicle.

The brave little racer set off. It bucked and bounced over this moraine, the engine barking and the suspension articulating wildly as Nick headed for easier ground. We had come through and this would be the start of many more adventures. Nick saw a market to this type of recreation and started his company 'Kankku,' which runs very successfully to this day. I have to say that this route is no longer open to vehicles, although some trail bikers still use it illegally.

We surveyed many more routes that summer. Nick acquired a Land Rover Discovery, which we would use as the pathfinder. So we often found ourselves in ridiculous situations that we would always solve. There was no stopping Fieldhouse now, he had Land Rover Defenders and Mitsubishi Pajeros in the Kankku fleet and punters were queuing up to be guided under instruction on how to properly drive off-road. Nick was very keen that clients behaved responsibly, they were taught how to respect the environment they were in. Any deviation from our instructions were very much frowned upon. Sometimes irresponsible drivers would be told to vacate their seats, one had to be strict, as the potential for danger was always present.

Dear Barty, who had worked with me at Eagle Quest, started instructing with us and worked for Nick for quite some time.

The National Park people were generally against this activity, but with Nick they met their match, with a barrister's mind he would have them scratching their heads. In fact, Nick has spent thousands of pounds and many hours repairing and improving those trails for the

Nick Fieldhouse's Kankku 4x4 vehicles driving from Tilberthwaite to little Langdale.

benefit of those who would oppose him. Shame on them, I say.

Nick, was now married with two lovely twins, Miles and Maisey. He also bought Windermere Auto Co. which enabled him to keep his off-road vehicles in good repair.

One day he went to a scrap yard in Keighley and bought a vintage machine, a 1946 Coles, which is an ex-RAF crane which lifts 10 tonnes. This he drove back to Windermere at the grand speed of 20 mph. At the grand age of 70 years old, she worked beautifully. She was mainly used for advertising purposes, but we would use her from time to time in various lifting jobs.

Nick also bought Nook End Farm, which is situated in an elevated position north of Ambleside. The views from the farm are stunning and it's one of my favourite places.

It was decided that a biomass boiler was needed to heat the property and a second hand one was acquired. The boiler was situated in an outbuilding on a farm in the Lythe Valley. In order to retrieve it we would have to remove some of the roof and lift it out. The old crane was cranked up and taken to the farm. The operation went well, the old crane worked beautifully, and the boiler and ancillary equipment was duly loaded onto trailers. It was decided that the crane should be driven straight to Nook End, but this would entail driving her up Nook Home, which is very narrow and we were not sure we could squeeze her through.

The road leading to Nook Lane is very steep (Smithy Brow) when a sharp corner leads into a narrow and winding lane, with steep walls on either side. Nick told me to make sure no vehicles were coming down as he approached. Three vans were coming as Nick was rounding the corner. No way could he have stopped, the brakes would never have held. I frantically managed to send the three of them into the green as Nick came, "chugity, chugity," ever so slowly into the narrows.

The lane was 8 feet wide, the crane was 8 feet wide, and the walls containing the lane were about 8 feet tall. No room for error! Nick was able to gauge the centre line. As I was to go in front, walking backwards indicating how much room we had at each side. Often there was none, as we scraped along, but somehow we never dislodged a single stone. This was team work indeed, and as the lane was about a quarter of a mile long, I was buggered as I stumbled backwards into the farmyard, and Nick with a huge grin of satisfaction on his face.

Nick, with the aid of dear Bruce Tomlinson and sometimes myself, was making a few alterations at Nook End. Field walls were being knocked down and relocated. Access roads were put in and fenced. The buildings were being repaired and altered to his needs. I enjoyed this kind of work, and although I'm feeling my age more and am not able to do quite so much as I did, I still enjoy it very much.

It was in my mind to start the conclusion to our little book when the phone rang. It was Jocky. "John," he said, "there is a lovely boat for sale at Glasson Dock, shall we go and have a look?" Well, having a look would do no harm, thought I, so within the hour he came by and picked me up and off we went to Glasson. Jocky, Katherine and I, just to go and have a look.

We rode in the old blue Land Rover, we were like the three musketeers off on another adventure, (maybe). As we pulled into the boatyard, we saw *Rosarne* standing there on her

Katherine and I sailing *Rosarne* from Glasson dock
to Maryport, moments before the force-9 blew in

bilge keels and looking magnificent. She is a 9-metre sloop, a Moody 31, her owner Vernon had sadly passed, so his family needed to sell her. His son greeted us and was understandably a little emotional, but as he showed us round, Jocks and I realised what a bargain she might be, if we could negotiate a good price. She had an incredible inventory, Jocky and I looked at each other. We were hooked. This boat was so well equipped and clearly diligently maintained by Vernon.

Susan, his widow, came to the boat yard with a bottle of champagne and we did the deal. She then said that Vernon had lots of stuff in the garage and could we take it away, so we opened the door we could not believe what lay before our eyes. It was as if we had walked into a ship's chandlery, the old Landy was well ladened when we left that place.

Part of the condition of sale was that we all meet up, once *Rosarne* was settled in her new home, and take the family, along with Vernon (ashes), when we can scatter him to the wind and tide. This we have yet to do.

At this time the lock gates, leading from the lagoon, were being repaired so it was not until the end of March that we were able to take her out to sea. On a lovely bright spring day Jocky, Katherine and I took advantage of the ebb tide down the Lune, which flushed us into Morecambe Bay. We headed north with an off-shore stiff breeze, the sails were full as we ran at full speed on a broad reach. We were so pleased dear old *Rosarne* was sailing beautifully as we set course for Maryport, which was to be her new home.

We had reached Lighting Knoll, at the southern end of Walney Island when a radio message came from Liverpool Coastguard on channel 16 warning to all shipping on the Irish Sea, "Gale force 9 imminent"! It arrived about half an hour later. It was a strong blow, but with sails reefed, dear old *Rosarne* sped along like a greyhound. (Vernon had always enjoyed sailing her in rough weather). By 10 o'clock that evening we rounded St Bees Head and passed through the lock gates at Whitehaven. We had been sailing for 10 hours and covered about 55 nautical miles. We berthed up, had supper and a huge night-cap and fell into a blissful sleep after an unforgettable day.

After breakfast, and waiting for the tide, we slipped the lock and headed for Maryport, about ten miles up the coast. Now this pretty little town, hosts a fantastic marina, and having once been a very important port, exporting iron and coal, and importing timber from North America and Canada. Ships were built here but trade declined when bigger iron steamers needed wider gates to get into the harbour. *Rosarne* now lives here in great luxury, just waiting for her next adventure. I wrote these few notes, perhaps as a preview, for the next seaborne tales I might have for my illustrious readers.

The dear old Golden Rule still remains a huge success and the wonderful staff, who mostly have been with me for many years, run the place. I still love to potter around, chatting with the customers and making them feel valued and welcome. It is people like you, my good readers, who make the pub what it is, and I thank you all for spending your time and money with us.

1 Fun gaggle flying above Keswick on a classic day
2 Sunset wow! Walla Crag, Keswick

3   Joc's boy Josh soaring on Skiddaw with Keswick below
4   Ballooning over the Langdales in kind conditions

1 Me with Becs
2 Me on John Street
3 The Golden Rule
4 Me and the lovely crypto, prior to losing thousands

5 Myself and Robert at the helm of the Gondola, 1991
6 Jocky, Johny and myself getting the last of the ale brewed at the Drunken Duck before it closed for lockdown, 2019
7 Rosie and I on Wrynose Pass, a super little dog

Margaret and I at the door of the pub during lockdown

1   With my dear friend Ans Khan, the bike came to me as part payment on a debt
2   The Coniston Steamer in modern times

CHAPTER 11

Mexico — To Find My Father

It was at the end of October 2022 when Jocky phoned me from Turkey. "John, he said, "we are going to Mexico in January, we need to find your father's resting place." He thought this would give me closure. I wasn't sure I needed this, but a Mexican adventure seemed like a great idea.

Jocky had been invited to direct a Mexican open paragliding competition at the Valle de Bravo, so after a drive to Heathrow, followed by a nine-hour night flight, we found ourselves in Mexico City.

We fetched up at our traditional colourful hotel at four o'clock am local time. We were very tired, but the hotel staff were kind enough to let us take our room immediately, so after a good nap and a late breakfast, we were ready to look for father's final resting place.

Unperturbed by the colossal amount of churches in Mexico City, we set about whittling down the locations of the churches where father's funeral might have been held. We decided that there were three Anglican churches that fitted the bill, by location of his house and work and also bearing in mind they were there at least 50 years ago. The first church we visited had been built in 1985 to replace an old church which had been demolished and which was closer to where father had worked. It was very beautiful, and the kind secretary told us the records of the old location had been saved and were available for our inspection.

Lo and behold, after ten minutes, we found the entry of the funeral in an old leather-bound register. From the record it showed that, after the ceremony, he had been taken to the British cemetery, cremated, and his ashes scattered in the garden. He loved Mexico, and this would have suited him well.

We had found him in the city of 20 million souls, and this happening so long ago. Clever stuff, eh? Seeing my father's name, and the details of his final movements, written in penned hand, did give me a feeling of peace, and I couldn't stop smiling. We went to the British cemetery and spent hours walking among the departed, resting in a foreign land, while the noise of city life drifted through the trees. We didn't find any plaque but it didn't matter, I knew he was scattered, right where I stood, so many years ago, and it did give me a gentle sense of closure.

Life moves at a fast pace in this huge metropolis, and although everything seems to be squeezed in, there are huge green areas where peace and quietness prevail. Chapultepec Park is a fine example, it is here where the National Museum of Anthropology is sited, a must for any visitor.

I had taken around 13,000 paces that day, taking in the history and atmosphere of this great city, and was quite happy when our car arrived the next morning to take us to Valle de Bravo.

Valle de Bravo, a beautiful holiday venue that sits on the Toluka plateau, is about 11,000 feet above sea level and about a four hour drive from Mexico City. One cannot help but notice the billions of dollars that have been spent on the transport infrastructure. Need a new motorway? Just build it above the old one, then build a railway above that. Common sense, eh?

The competition organisers in the Valle de Bravo were wonderful, we were provided with a jeep and were treated like royalty. It was a big competition with 150 pilots taking part over a period of five days. These were cross country tasks, each of about 100km in distance with a set goal, and turn points to be negotiated during the flight, about 60–80 % of pilots would fall by the wayside to be picked up by the retrieve buses. Even so, points would be awarded for the distance achieved.

When the team were marking out the scores at the end of the day, I would go off to a little bar for a gin and tonic, a nice quiet time for me, where I could sit, reflect on the day, and watch the beautiful sunsets form over the lake. Walking back to the office on the fourth evening I missed a step and popped my sciatic nerve. The pain was so intense, I could not move for several minutes. Paracetamol and pain relief patches did little to help, so I suffered it with the aid of a walking stick and helpful friends until our return to England. Back home, diazepam and codeine did the trick.

The competition was a huge success and was closed with a prize-giving gala, and afterwards at a top restaurant where I had the best fillet steak I have ever eaten, washed down with a 40-year-old tequila, smooth as any cognac. Having said farewell to our wonderful hosts, we took a plane down to Cancun for a little seaside treat.

Only too soon, we were on our way back to Mexico City and preparing to leave for England. I was pensive leaving Mexico. I felt comfortable there, it had been over 60 years since my last visit with Philip, and although much has changed, I couldn't help but feel that the hospitable soul of the place still remained. It was also good to know that I had found my father and I could share this news with my family at home.

My friendship with Jocky has allowed me to visit so many countries and to meet such interesting and diverse people. I deem myself a lucky man.

Proudly holding my father's log, No 9

1

2

1 New Anglican church
2 Me admiring the fine architecture
3 Valle de Bravo, Mexico
4 Competition glide
5 Me reflecting on past times

(All photos in this chapter by J Sanderson)

trust and affection for each other, we look forward to many more adventures together. I am sure, my dear readers, that you will read more of these in the future.

I have to mention Nick Fieldhouse and his delightful children, Miles and Maisy. I have worked with Nick for decades, I admire and respect him, and enjoy spending time with him, and the family, at Nook End farm.

Dear Johnny Wrennall came to work with me 18 years ago, he has managed the business impeccably, and has been a true and dear friend to me. Without his help I think I would have retired some years ago, I will be ever grateful to him.

These dear people are just a few who have shaped my life. There are many, many more and I am sorry I haven't named them here, as my little book would have then turned into a big book.

1   Me sailing *Elizabeth Anne* back from Kirkudbright

\>   Jocky and I splicing the main braise

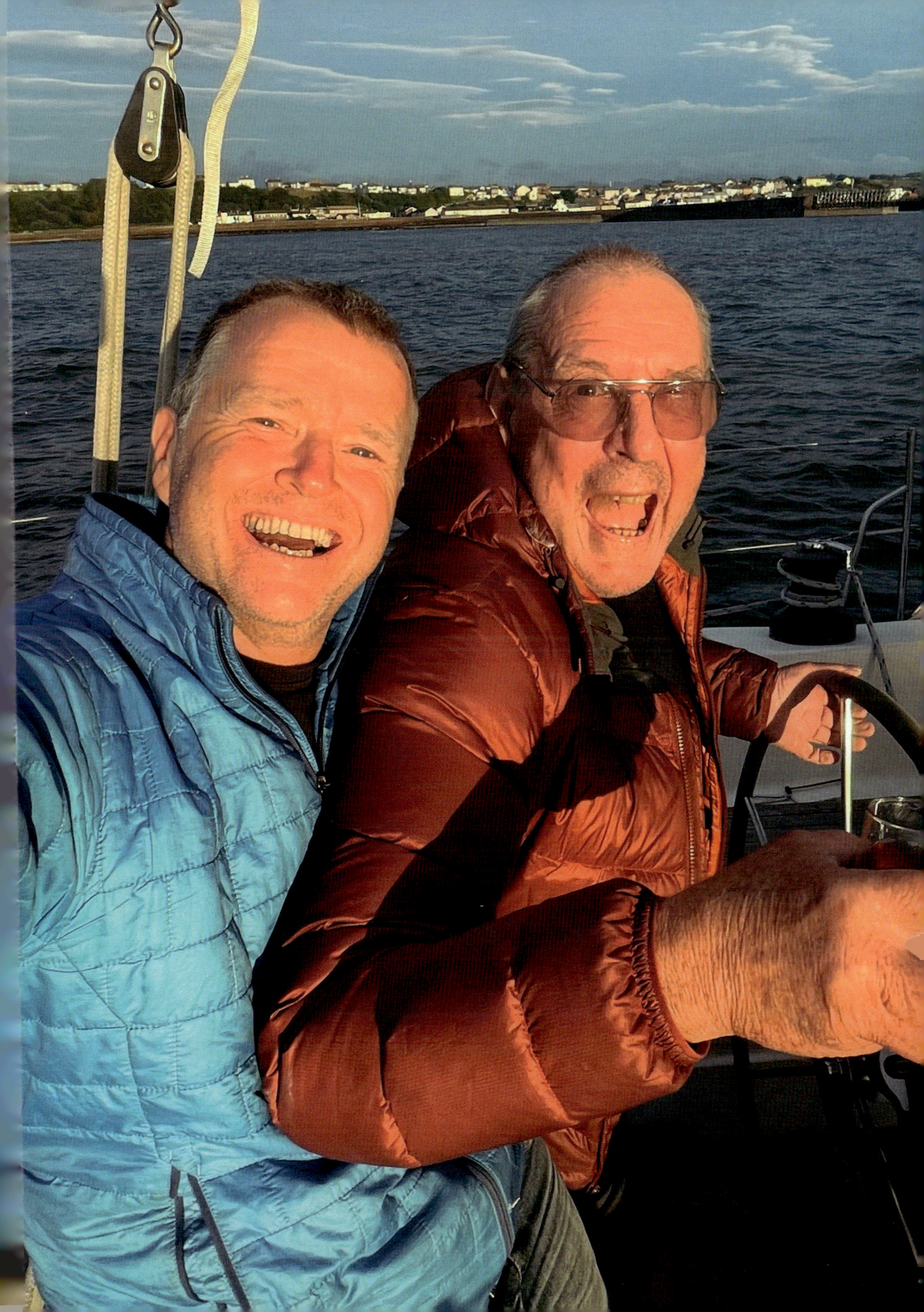

The Golden Rule

by

Hope Elegia Wandless

Your red chipped old wooden door
Holds up your aging stonework,
A golden haze, a dizzy blonde hue.
The smell of pints being pulled
In the glow of the roaring fire.

A resting place for the weary, the wanderers.
The wondering soul will soon find refuge
With a glass of red or the hoppiest ale that
Money can buy.

Your walls whisper the memories of three centuries,
A starstruck legacy standing amongst the fells,
Those nights where the conversation flowed
Long after the beer.

The stories hang, oil paint history,
The memory of tobacco smoke
still wafting through the rooms.
The familiar feeling of warmth,
Not from the fire, but from the people.

The man with the eyepatch; his tankard and tin can change,
The tourists who talk football with me over the bar,
And my regulars who mock my plaid trousers on Mondays and Sundays.

This Rule is a heart
Beating life through this Lakeland town.
The life that leads to each other in this
home brewed community.

Hope works for me, she's a lovely young lady who writes beautiful poems. Her work will become well known in the future.

Julian Heaton Cooper, of Cooper dynasty, painted this picture of the bar in 1995. A famous landscape artist, this little picture was one of four atypical of his real work. I paid him £400 for it at the time.